MW00873146

In Recovery

Courtney Pankrat

In Plain Sight Publishing
2019

Published by:
In Plain Sight Publishing
Denver, Colorado 80247

Copyright © Courtney Pankrat
All rights reserved. No part of this book may be reproduced, scanned, or
distributed in any printed or electronic form without permission. Please do
not participate in or encourage piracy of copyrighted materials in violation of
the authors' rights. Purchase only authorized editions.

Library of Congress Cataloging-in-Publication Data

Pankrat, Courtney
In Recovery: Stories of Healing from Mental Illness

pages cm
Includes bibliographical references.
ISBN 978-0-359-92794-4 (Paperback)
1. Psychology   2. Mental Health   3. Memoir

Book design by Courtney Pankrat

For Johanna,
I wouldn't be here
without you.

Table of contents

Introduction

Words are important. I had to weigh every word in this book because I wanted to make sure that each participant's story was told in a fair and honest manner without being overly triggering to readers. I wanted to be very careful in the way I represented each participant. Each of these brave people has allowed me to tell their story and I wanted to represent them as authentically as possible.

When I was deep in my suffering from mental illness, I would often read books about people with my illness and be encouraged to get as ill as the person in the book, or I would compare myself to the person. Talking about behaviors people exhibit in their illnesses makes for interesting reading, but that reading is not healing. That being said, this book does describe mental illness in some detail. If you feel triggered while reading any part of it, please talk to a therapist. Without fail, when every participant was in their illness, they were miserable, even though it may not have looked that way.

I tried to make this book one that I would have not only liked to have read when I was suffering from mental illness, but also one that would have been beneficial to my healing.

I named this book In Recovery because I wanted to illustrate that recovery looks different for everyone and even looks different for each person at various times in their life. Being in recovery is not synonymous with having recovered. Having recovered from an illness implies that it's over, never to be thought of again. I look at recovery as an ongoing journey. Some days are better than others. For me, my only requirement for being in recovery is that I'm doing the best I can. I am showing up.

Some participants very clearly expressed the belief that they are not their illness; their illness does not define them. Others took the opposite point of view: they are who they are today because of, despite, and thanks to their illness.

The stories in this book have many things in common and also many differences. Some participants recovered using traditional methods such as talk therapy and medication. Others found alternative methods to be more helpful. Each person's story is unique, and hopefully every reader will be able to find commonality with at least one of the stories.

This book is meant to inspire people who are currently suffering from mental illness. I want you to know that you are not alone, even though it often feels that way. I know it does. I understand. When you are ready to ask for help, you will be able to find it.

Each chapter of this book highlights a different participant's journey, retelling the story they shared with me when I interviewed them. After the courageous participants told me their stories, I compiled and edited each one. I wanted every participant to be proud of their part in this book. With that in mind, all have had a chance to read their story and offer comments and edits to it. At the end of the book, I've outlined the coping skills and tips the participants shared with me. I then shared other books that have been meaningful to participants in the book.

Lauren Murphy

Lauren and I became friends under unusual circum-stances. She was my roommate in rehab. When I went to rehab in 2005, I was severely depressed, amongst other things, and I was not there to make friends. I slept for the first four days but eventually had to start participating.

When I was moved to a permanent room and was as-signed Lauren as my roommate, I was not thrilled. She was clearly one of the "cool kids" and I just didn't have the energy to try to impress her. I should have realized that since she was also in rehab, she wasn't in the great-est place in her life, but I was too self-absorbed to think about this. Mainly, I worried that she would be mean to me. I was already very broken and couldn't handle much criticism.

It didn't take long for me to realize how wrong I was about Lauren. Yes, she was cool and well liked amongst the other patients. She was also kind, funny, willing to listen, and generous with advice. Our struggles and past experiences differed greatly, yet over the weeks we spent together, I grew to love her in a way that has been rare for me in my life.

—

Lauren's troubles started long before we met and con-tinued for years afterwards. She has always lived life to the fullest, in ways both positive and negative.

Lauren grew up in Alaska. She describes her childhood as a mixture of good and bad. Her parents divorced when she was a toddler, and her mother eventually remarried. Lauren recalls that both of her parents often abused al-cohol.

When Lauren was 11 years old, her father, a lawyer, was

working on getting his pilot's license and was killed in a plane crash. This tragic loss at such a young age would be one of the roots of Lauren's future suffering. "They say that when girls lose their father, especially around puberty, [they] end up being way more prone to eating disorders," Lauren says. "They are more prone to suicide and depression, and they end up in more abusive relationships."

"When my dad died it was awful, but we didn't have the worst childhood," she says. "It certainly wasn't the best, but we were never hungry, we never wanted for anything." After her father's death, Lauren lived full-time with her mother. Lauren's mother eventually got sober and left her second husband, both events that Lauren describes as good.

However, Lauren struggled. She was only 12 years old when her mom first checked her into a mental health crisis institution. She recalls that she liked being there. She found it easy and learned that she could get away with a lot. "You could go there, and go to group and say whatever, and you could act out and everyone was like, 'oh, it's okay,'" she says.

Lauren started experimenting with drugs and alcohol and ran into addiction problems while she was still in high school. She dropped out of school at 16, got her GED, and started working at a dead-end job for little pay.

When she was 17, Lauren gave birth to her son, Max. She was able to get sober while she was pregnant but relapsed soon after giving birth. "I think I knew at the time that I was a drug addict," Lauren says. "I didn't care. I thought I could beat it and I liked using. I felt like I was good at it. I liked the lifestyle. I liked the people that I hung out with. I understood them. They were my people. I felt pretty comfortable drinking and using even though it really destroyed my life."

After Max was born, Lauren's life was tumultuous. "I was supposed to be an adult, but I was still a kid," she says. Her relationship with Max's father was a mess. "We were together, but we were together in the way that 17-year-old kids are together." The two didn't have a good relationship and Lauren often felt like she had two children to take care of.

When Max was around 2 years old, Lauren moved to California to go to college and Max stayed back with Lauren's mom in Alaska. Lauren lived with her aunt and uncle while she was in school and initially, she got good grades. She was still drinking and using drugs heavily though, and her aunt and uncle eventually checked her into her first rehab center. She was only 19.

This was the beginning of a two-year stretch of time where Lauren jumped around from one treatment center to another. Inevitably, she would get drunk or use drugs and get kicked out.

"I never graduated a treatment center for drugs and alcohol," Lauren recalls. After getting kicked out of yet another treatment center, when she was 21, Lauren moved back to Alaska and decided to try Alcoholics Anonymous (AA). She started going to meetings regularly and found a sponsor, Connie, who she clicked with. "I didn't expect to [like AA] but it worked really well for me," Lauren says.

With Connie's help, Lauren got sober. She worked hard at the 12 steps of the AA program and made good friends in the group. "It was so fun," she says. "I could spend my whole day with people from AA, running around, going to the movies, getting coffee, going to each other's houses, going to more meetings." That comradery helped Lauren stay sober.

After being sober for a few months, she and Connie started looking at her eating habits and realized that she had a problem. She'd had an eating disorder since she was young, but her alcoholism and drug addiction were more visible to the outside world and a more pressing problem at the time.

Connie and Lauren tried to apply the AA steps to her eating disorder. But Connie wasn't an expert and it soon became clear that Lauren needed more help than Connie was able to provide.

Lauren felt lucky to have access to Rosewood Ranch, an eating disorder treatment center in Wickenburg, Arizona. Her treatment was covered by her health insurance and she knew she needed to go. "It was kind of humiliating because everybody at work found out what was going on and that sucked, but it was worth it because I got to go to Rosewood," Lauren recalls.

Lauren learned a lot about food and coping skills in treatment while her body recovered from the physical effects of her eating disorder. She stopped all her disordered behaviors and her body normalized, at least while she was in the treatment center. "I was still bat-shit crazy," Lauren says. "It wasn't an overnight thing, or even a 30-day thing. It was like, slowly, it started getting better."

For Lauren, bulimia was a very different beast than drug and alcohol addiction. "I really didn't want to have an eating disorder. I would rather be an alcoholic or a drug addict. I felt more comfortable in that space. Having an eating disorder does make sense in my addiction, but I didn't enjoy it," she says.

She recalls that getting drunk with her friends may have led to some embarrassing moments but that the next day everyone would have a good laugh about it. While she might have felt ashamed of her drunken behavior, getting drunk or high seemed much more socially acceptable than bingeing and purging. Bulimia is "really a shameful thing and people are really weird about it. They don't understand it," Lauren says.

By the time Lauren went to Rosewood at 21 years old, she wanted to be better. "Rosewood was one of the only places I ever went with the intent of getting better," she says. "I was there on business. I was ready to take whatever tools I could. I'd never done that before."

Lauren did well at Rosewood. It was the only treatment center in which she didn't use drugs or alcohol, and the only center she didn't get kicked out of. Even though she continued to struggle after leaving, Rosewood was the beginning of her upward progression.

—

Lauren continued to work on her recovery and sobriety for the next few years. At the age of 25, she was four years sober. She married a man named Ryan. Right from the start, there were problems in their marriage and within less than one month, Lauren had given up her of sobriety.

"I married a guy that was a total asshole. He was really religious, and he was very abrasive and straightforward," Lauren says. "For some reason I thought that was a good thing. I thought, 'here's a guy that tells it like it is. He's always going to be honest with me.' He was honest but he was also a fucking asshole. He treated me like shit, and he treated Max like shit. He would often quote the Bible or quote some religious idea to justify his behavior."

The hard work Lauren had put into getting sober collapsed and she started drinking and having affairs. "I didn't know it at the time, but looking back, I see I was really miserable," Lauren says. "I didn't want to be married. Actually, I didn't want to be married to that guy." The marriage fell apart quickly. It was over in less than a year.

Around the time she and Ryan got married, Lauren enrolled in nursing school. She earned a scholarship and initially thrived in her classes, just as she had the previous time she'd been to college.

However, she soon discovered that nursing was not for her. While there are many different types of jobs in nursing, she says, "I didn't realize how much of it was working with sick people. Not even that, but sick and miserable people." Lauren found that not only were patients and their families unhappy, a lot of nurses were miserable as well. She realized that being a nurse wasn't the life she wanted for herself.

—

Throughout Lauren's struggles, Max was growing up. He lived with Lauren's mother most of the time until he turned five. Eventually, Lauren was able to care for him, and he moved back in with her. He lived with her while she was married to Ryan and Lauren still worries about long-term damage this had on Max. She doesn't only blame Ryan, recognizing that she chose to leave Max alone with Ryan while she went out to bars at night.

In 2009, in an effort to get Max involved in an activity, Lauren took him to a Jiu-Jitsu class. She had always wanted to try martial arts, and she wanted to give her son the opportunity she never had. Max didn't like it. Lauren, however, fell in love with the sport and started taking classes.

Ryan hated that Lauren was practicing martial arts, which she says was just one more thing that drove them apart. She would come home from practice feeling excited and empowered. Initially she wanted to share this excitement with Ryan, but he was dismissive. He started taking Kung Fu and would minimize her experiences in Jiu-Jitsu by telling her that his sport was superior. Jiu-Jitsu "gave me a new confidence away from Ryan and he really fucking did not like it," Lauren says.

Jiu-Jitsu didn't come easily to Lauren. "It was really humbling," Lauren remembers. "I was really bad, but I wanted to be better."

She was no stranger to physical activity, but she'd never been on a team, nor had she competed in a sport. "That was all new to me. I wanted to be better, so I had to show up every day." Jiu-Jitsu became a catalyst for change in Lauren's life. Instead of just working out like she'd done in the past, she was now on a great team that she loved.

—

Meanwhile, Lauren's marriage continued to dissolve. She recounts times when Ryan quoted the Bible to support his views that women should be submissive to their husbands and put their husbands above all else, even their children. Lauren believed Ryan when he told her that this was what God wanted.

"I thought that he must know and that I must be an idiot," she says. "I thought that I was so fucked up that I couldn't even [trust] what I thought or felt." She now recognizes that this kind of thinking is unsound, but she also acknowledges that it's very common.

Years after her divorce, Lauren recalls Ryan's behavior like this: "I don't think he was intentionally abusive. I think that he had some things going on from his childhood and he had just learned these behaviors. He thought what he was doing was the way marriage was supposed to be."

Near the end of her relationship with Ryan, Lauren fell for someone new. "I don't know why I was crazy about him," she says. "He wasn't any better. He was just another Ryan, but [falling for him] made it easier to leave the relationship with Ryan."

—

Meanwhile, Max was struggling. He had no stability in his life. Lauren had started dating this new man and was getting evicted from her apartment. She made some money working odd jobs but any money she made she spent at bars, drinking. She knew she couldn't take care of Max.

Lauren called Max's father and asked him for help. She didn't know where she was going to live after her eviction, and she wanted Max to have a safe place to live. Max's father was able to provide that for him. He also had a nice girlfriend at the time who Lauren felt was good for Max.

While Lauren was going downhill, she still made as much of an effort to see Max as she could. However, she admits that she wasn't in a good place. It is obvious that she still feels guilty about how she couldn't be there for her son during that time.

—

On Lauren's 27th birthday, she went out to celebrate with some friends from Jiu-Jitsu. She drank a lot and got behind the wheel. At the time, she was in a total blackout. "I don't remember even getting in my car," she says.

She got pulled over for going over 100 miles per hour down the freeway at three o'clock in the morning. Lauren refused a breathalyzer test, which she doesn't advise, as along with the refusal comes additional charges. She was taken to jail for a few days.

During that first night in jail, she knew her life would never be the same. "I remember just lying there in the cell and watching the clock until it was seven o'clock in the morning and thinking, 'fuck, my whole life is about to change.'" Her night in jail meant that she would officially get kicked out of nursing school because she would have to miss a required course. This was the last straw for Lauren.

One of Lauren's friends from the gym was a man named Joe. She approached him after her DUI and asked him for help. She asked if he would take her to an AA meeting. Lauren spent the next few weeks sleeping on friends' couches and going to meetings. She felt like she had once again reached rock bottom. "It was like when I was 19," Lauren says.

Lauren and Joe eventually started dating and the two quickly fell in love. Lauren describes the first six months of their relationship as hellish since she was in the process of getting sober. Slowly but surely, though, Lauren got her life together. She was in a low place: she'd lost her driver's license, she was in debt with student loans and court fees totaling almost $100,000, and she needed a job.

—

In the summer of 2012, Lauren applied to be a member of a traveling wildfire firefighter crew. Because the crew traveled often, she wouldn't need an apartment. She could stay with Joe when she was in Anchorage.

Working on the fire crew was grueling. The crew mainly stayed in Alaska but would fly out to assist when other crews around the country needed help.

Wildfire crews do important work, especially in areas where wilderness abounds, like Alaska. Unfortunately, Lauren's experience with the fire crew was not good. Her teammates would constantly bring each other down by making fun of and belittling each other. The work itself was the hardest thing Lauren had ever done; being in a negative environment with bullies did not make it easier.

Even though the experience was awful, Lauren learned a valuable life lesson. Around the end of the summer, a few new people joined her crew, and they were not yet as physically fit as the other crew members.

The experienced members didn't go easy on the newbies. They made one of the new guys carry the five-gallon water jug that everyone drank from. Lauren recalls that the crew was going up a mountain one day and everyone was struggling as the air thinned out. The men on the team were calling the new kid names and telling him how much he sucked.

Eventually, the new kid broke down in tears. Lauren stayed silent but another woman, who was also new to the crew, stood up for him. "She said: 'you guys need to shut the fuck up,'" Lauren recalls. "'If you are going to be making fun of him, then you should be making fun of me too. We are all dying on this crew today.'"

The woman didn't stick around on the team for very long, but she made a huge impression on Lauren. Lauren realized that she wanted to be someone who stood up for others too. The men on the crew hated the woman who stood up to them, but Lauren knew that what she'd said was true. "That poor kid was fucking doing his best and he was doing a job that nobody else wanted to do," Lauren says. "Instead of lifting him up, telling him 'good job,' and making him feel like part of the team, everybody just beat him down."

—

After her summer on the fire crew, Lauren moved in with Joe in Alaska. Before long, though, he was transferred to Florida with his job in the military. Lauren knew that she could not lose Joe. The two were in love and she wanted to marry him. Joe was different from all the other men Lauren had ever dated. He was kind to her, and he respected her. Lauren hadn't ever believed in soulmates until she met Joe, and she wasn't interested in being away from him. She decided to move with him to Florida.

Even though Max didn't live with Lauren at the time, her family, friends, and Max's father were angry that she would leave without Max. They didn't understand how she could leave her son behind. But to Lauren, this was not only something she needed to do, she knew it was the right thing to do. "Joe was the best thing that ever happened to me and I couldn't let him go," she says. She knew that if she stayed behind in Alaska, she would continue her cycle of self-destructive behavior.

—

Joe and Lauren got married in Florida in 2013. Lauren got more serious about martial arts and launched her mixed martial arts (MMA) career. That same year, Lauren competed in eight MMA fights and won them all. She was soon asked to join the Ultimate Fighting Championship (UFC) league, the top league in her sport. She started fighting with the league in July 2014.

Lauren trained at a small gym in Houston, Texas. She'd drive the eight hours from her home in Florida for training camps and would sometimes stay in Houston for two to three months while she trained for a fight. After each fight, she would spend a few weeks back at home in Florida, before returning to train for the next fight. This went on for about a year. When Joe eventually left the military, the couple got to choose where they wanted to live.

The two found a few cities they liked and that had good MMA gyms. After visiting different gyms and meeting with coaches, they decided to move to Phoenix, Arizona. After living in Alaska for most of her life, Phoenix's warm climate was also a key factor in the decision.

The next step for the couple was to get Max back. Lauren was now sober and thriving in her MMA career. Initially, she thought that Max was happy living with his father, but it later became clear that things were not going well for her son.

Max's father had a good job, and everyone liked him, but he was controlling. Max was exhibiting some unusual behavior at the time. Lauren didn't understand it until she investigated his counseling records and realized that his life with his dad wasn't as healthy as she thought. At that point, she decided to fight hard to regain custody of her son.

The custody battle was difficult and long. After winning one of her MMA fights, Lauren had enough money to hire a lawyer. She eventually won full custody of Max, and he moved to Phoenix to live with her and Joe.

—

Lauren has had to work hard to make her MMA career a positive experience. She says she used to be obsessively negative. "Nothing was ever good enough. I wasn't good enough. And if I didn't work out one day, [I thought] I wouldn't be good enough," she says.

Through practice and meditation, Lauren realized that there was a way for her to be both obsessive and positive. "You can be obsessive and still think, 'that was a great workout and I'm getting so much better,'" she says. "Or, 'wow, what a great learning experience.' It's all about practice and trial and error."

When Lauren first started to compete in professional sports, she was extremely focused on winning and losing. "I couldn't imagine anything more humiliating or awful than losing, which is ridiculous. There are plenty of things that are way fucking worse than losing at a sport," she says. She didn't deal with her losses very well because she'd tied her identity to the results of her fights.

Even though she'd made it to the UFC, she still had doubts about whether she belonged. For the first time, she lost some fights, and her self-doubt grew. "You just got here because you are lucky. You're not really that talented," she would think to herself. Despite being in the toughest and most highly respected league in her sport, she felt embarrassed and ashamed.

The UFC hosts a reality TV show called The Ultimate Fighter. Each season of the show features MMA athletes and follows them throughout their practices and fights while the athletes live together in a community house. The 26th season of the show focused on a new flyweight women's bracket.

Lauren fought in the featherweight division but knew she could also be competitive in the flyweight division. Lauren was asked to participate in the show and was seated third in the competition. She thought it was her turn to win but she lost her first fight at the house. Again, she was filled with self-doubt.

—

Recently, Lauren has had a big win and a big loss in the UFC, and her perspective has changed. "Maybe I'm not the best fighter, but I'm definitely not the worst," she says. "I'm going to take this as far as I can possibly go and there's no shame in that anymore." No matter what happens, Lauren will always know that she won two fights[1] in the UFC and she can feel proud of herself for that.

While plenty of people judge her and throw insults her way, Lauren has realized that their behavior says more about them than it does about her. "I never used to think that," she says. If someone told her she sucked, she believed them. She feels that her newfound outlook is a result of having had some time to grow up and mature.

Lauren has learned many lessons in a much more public way than most of us. Her UFC fights are televised, so she has had to deal with losing in front of a large audience, and she is a public figure on social media. She hasn't ever done things the easy way. "The fire crew was difficult, fighting is difficult, getting sober was difficult," she says. Even as he handed Lauren a stripe on her purple belt, her Jiu-Jitsu coach told her: "You have earned every bit of

---

1   She's since won a third fight in August 2019.

this. Sometimes you just make things harder on yourself than you need to," she recalls.

—

During our conversation, Lauren and I discuss what has helped her the most. Her first response is MMA. The routine of having practice every day and at the same time really helps her. She feels that if she wants to be any good, she has to go to practice, and she wants to be good. The structure and purpose of MMA also help her even out her eating habits. "I didn't want to just be skinny anymore. I wanted to be strong. I wanted to be healthy so that I could compete well," she says.

Lauren no longer thinks of her body as an ornament for people to judge; she now sees it as a vehicle. She used to like the attention she would get for being thin. It gave her a sense of power. Now, though, she's using her body for something she values. "I want to be a world champion, and to me that's more important [than being thin]," Lauren says.

Her new body also attracts attention. People often approach her and tell her how huge her arms are, and she gets attacked online about the way she looks. These comments do still affect her. However, once she realized that she can't please everyone no matter what she does, she was able to let go of the shame. "If you're fat, you're too fat, if you are skinny, you're too skinny, if you are muscular, you are too muscular. It's always fucking something, you know?" Lauren says. "I think it's important to realize that the only person whose opinion truly matters is my own. I have to be comfortable and happy and healthy in my own life. It makes no sense to live my life for someone else's opinion."

Lauren's relationship with Joe has also helped her immensely in her recovery. She has a healthy outlook on their relationship. They have a wonderful life together, but they also have their own lives. They support each other no matter what, but they aren't always involved in what the other person is doing.

"We made it a point from the very beginning to be honest with each other about everything," Lauren says. She admits that they still have their moments, but overall, they have a very strong relationship.

Lauren credits AA for a lot of her recovery. Working the 12 steps has helped her look at herself honestly. She doesn't go to meetings often anymore. She's started using marijuana to help with her anxiety and insomnia, which is frowned upon in AA. For Lauren, marijuana helps her feel more positive and happier in general. "I think it makes me see things in a different way than I normally would," she says. Furthermore, Lauren never found another sponsor with whom she clicked as she did with Connie.

While she has found a meeting in Arizona that she likes, she recognizes that AA is different for her now. Many people in AA are very ill, and Lauren is in a different place in her life. However, she still uses the 12 steps in her daily life.

Another lesson Lauren has learned is that not every problem necessarily requires a big intervention or life change. For someone used to doing everything at 100%, this concept has been an important realization.

Lauren has a strong community in her MMA team. "I think a lot of times, people with eating disorders, and people with drug addictions, or alcoholics, whatever it is,

I think they feel so lonely," Lauren explains. "Have you heard of rat park?"[2] she asks excitedly. She's referring to a 1978 experiment that found that rats drank significantly more morphine solution when isolated than when kept in a "park" that offered mental stimulation and the company of other rats. Lauren says the study's implication rings true for humans, too: "when you are surrounded by community and people you love and support, you make a lot of better decisions for yourself."

Lauren dealt with loneliness a lot when she was suffering from bulimia. She felt that nobody understood her and that she couldn't confide in anyone. "I was so ashamed; I didn't want to tell anybody. I felt like everybody knew and they were all judging me," she says. "But I think with community and a feeling of belonging, people can overcome amazing things."

—

Max, Lauren, and Joe have lived together in Phoenix since 2014. Joe recently finished his undergraduate degree, is the general manager at the gym where Lauren trains, and is a black belt in Judo and Jiu-Jitsu. Max is finishing high school and exploring college options.

Lauren's overall professional fighting record is 10-4.[3] Lauren knows that she will not be a professional fighter forever, and at 36 years old, she is one of the league's older competitors. She has started studying to get an undergraduate degree in nutrition.

A counselor recently told Lauren that there are four important things people need in life: a mentor, a best friend, a purpose, and a passion. Your mentor and best friend

---

2   Alexander, B.K., Coambs, R.B. & Hadaway, P.F. Psychopharmacology (1978) 58: 175. https://doi.org/10.1007/BF00426903
3   Her recent UFC win has changed her record to 11-4.

should not be the same person. Your purpose and your passion should also not be the same thing. Lauren says her mentor is her coach and her best friend is Joe. She believes her purpose is to help people, and she wants to accomplish this through nutrition counselling. Lauren's passion is MMA. She says she is fortunate to be able to make her living through her passion for now, and she plans to participate in MMA in some capacity long after she finishes making money as a professional athlete.

When Lauren reflects on her recovery journey, she remembers that it seemed endless and that she would never get better. But slowly, she did get better. She still obsesses sometimes, but for the most part, she understands that life doesn't need to be so complicated.

—

Since Lauren and I spoke, she competed in another UFC fight. After taking a break to recovery from foot surgery, Lauren fought Italian fighter Mara Romero Borella in New Jersey on August 3, 2019. She won the fight by technical knockout (TKO) in the third round making her record 11-4. Not only did she win the fight, she looked more confident than ever in the octagon. She is now ranked ninth in the UFC's flyweight division. She is taking some well-deserved rest time before training for the next fight.

Ali Baylor

Ali and I met in 2012. We were both part of an ecotherapy certification program offered by John F. Kennedy University in California. Most of the classes were online, so we didn't meet until the end of the program. At the time, I was participating in the program as part of my master's degree in psychology. I was keen on learning about ecotherapy, a field of therapy that encourages people to interact with nature as a way to stay emotionally healthy but didn't understand how to use it in practice. Ali was way ahead of me. She was already working as an ecotherapist at her ranch in Brooksville, Florida. She probably could have taught some of the courses in the certification program.

I always thought of Ali as a healer. I learned during our time in the program that she takes care of her husband, David, who has been severely ill for many years, and that she spends most of her time caring for others as the owner and operator of the ranch.

It wasn't until I started to write this book that I learned about Ali's past struggles in life. We met at her ranch in June 2018, where she took the time to show me around, introduced me to her husband, and told me her story.

—

Ali was born in Massachusetts and moved to Florida when she was 7 years old. Her mom was a lawyer and her father, a doctor. She has one brother who she describes as very organized. "He came out just like my mom," Ali says. "He's a lawyer too, just like she was. My mom was brave — one of the first women teaching fellows at Harvard Law, very into women's rights, extremely bright. On the surface she was really amazing, but she was a terrible mother," Ali reflects.

Ali sees more of herself in her father. He taught her empathy and a heart-based way of looking at the world. "He worked his ass off. He grew up poor and got a scholarship to Harvard. He was the kindest, most caring doctor who actually prayed with people, and started a foundation for spirituality in healing," she says.

The move to Florida came after Ali's parents visited on vacation. Her father was in the early stages of his medical career in oncology and the family decided that he would start his practice in Florida.

Ali grew up in a house in Belleair, which was a rich neighborhood: "lots of upper middle-class status symbols and entitled people with designer clothing," she says. She never felt like she fit in because those things seemed unimportant to her.

Though Ali had her first depressive episode in college, she believes her depression began when she was much younger. She was in therapy at age 13. "I was just a wreck in middle school. I think my suicide attempt with a bottle of aspirin was more of a cry for help," Ali recalls.

When she was in high school, things seemed to calm down a bit. "I thought I was doing pretty well," she remembers. She went to Harvard, just as her father had, but within six months she fell into a depression.

Not knowing how to cope, Ali slept around a lot in college. "I didn't know what to do. I was so disconnected from everyone. Sleeping around, smoking a lot of pot, and becoming bulimic — those were the only coping mechanisms that I had. It was right before the AIDS [epidemic] took off. The possibility of getting AIDS scared the crap out of me and that was the end of the promiscuity," Ali says.

After college, Ali moved back to Florida and got engaged twice before she met David. She described both men as good guys, but meek guys who she could push around. "I didn't love or respect either of them. I think I just wanted to be married," she says.

Less than a year after breaking off the second engagement, Ali met David. It was January 2000 and Ali taught seventh-grade life sciences. David was a sixth-grade geography teacher. The two had grown up in the same area in Florida, but since David was older than Ali, they had never crossed paths. Not long after they met, Ali moved in with David. They lived in a small house in a rainbow neighborhood, not the upper middle-class environment she was used to, which suited her well.

Ali's family's reaction to her relationship with David was unusual. "I remember my brother sitting on the couch with David and saying, 'can you tell me what you're doing with my sister? She's damaged goods. You don't want her.' Both my brother and mother referred to me as 'damaged goods,'" Ali says. "David helped me stand up to everybody. By the end of my mom's life in 2006, she loved and accepted David, and realized that his unconditional love was the best thing for me."

"I know my mom loved me and wanted to protect me, but she was afraid of anything unknown or spontaneous. She was so afraid of me failing, me not turning out the way she wanted me to, me not being happy. My problems always reminded her of her poor parenting abilities. But she could never do therapy with me. She lived with that guilt until she died," Ali reflects.

"I couldn't cut my mother out. I did end up seeing a therapist who helped me stop seeing myself through my mother's eyes, and instead through David's eyes," Ali says. "And now I see myself clearly with my own eyes. I love me. Finally."

—

David got sick soon after the pair got together and had to stop teaching. David was diagnosed with a benign brain tumor in 2001. The tumor was surgically removed but returned two years later and was inoperable this time. He was given 12 months to live. While the tumor couldn't be removed, radiation therapy was an option, albeit a dangerous one.

In 2005, the family decided to move forward with the radiation after much agonizing deliberation. David's radiation was successful in that it eradicated the tumor, but it also took his entire pituitary gland. He started total hormone replacement therapy, which involved a timer, a pillbox, and lots of nagging, Ali says.

—

When Ali's mom died, she left Ali a sum of money. Ali and David used that money to move from the suburbs to the country and grow their own food, thinking it would be helpful for David's health.

"The original plan for moving to [a property with] 10 acres was to grow all our own food. That didn't work out completely, but we did do some veggies, eggs, and beef," Ali explains. "But by the time we butchered the third cow we didn't want to do it anymore. We fell in love with our cows, and now only have two rescue cows who are infertile. We get our meat at Whole Foods."

Around this time, Ali's father moved in with her and David. He'd only been living with them for six months when he attempted suicide. Ali found him after his attempt. "It was horrible," she recalls. "He felt guilty. He felt he was ruining our lives by living with us." Her father now lives only 10 minutes away in an assisted living facility. "I think it's better that he's there now. He needs a lot of taking care of and he comes over here now and things are good when he does."

"The whole time we've been at the ranch, we've always known that David could die at any time," Ali says. "I've had to live the entire 18 years that we've been together knowing that."

Ali has had to work to see the bright side of living with the man she loves while knowing that any given day could be their last day together. "In a way it's been great for me," Ali says. "I would say that that's what made me thrive in crisis, because I had to step up and accept that I only have a short time. David is terminal. But we all are, really. Each day could be anyone's last. Living with this illness has taught me to live in the present and stop worrying about things beyond my control."

Every once in a while, Ali gets down about it and sometimes her meds need adjusting. Both Ali and her dad suffer from bipolar disorder. "We have both had to learn to work with the ups and downs," she says. "But everyone is flawed and emotionally scarred; every human being has to deal with pain and heartbreak. This is what makes us appreciate the good times."

As is common, Ali has had to try many different medications before she found the right combination. She is on several medications now that have worked well for the past 10 years. "The only times I was ever manic were the first time I went on Prozac, and one other time when I went to a sleepaway camp and I didn't get enough sleep,"

Ali says. "I've definitely had 'up' days, but no severe manic episodes."

Ali admits that the depression is harder to beat, it sneaks in even with effective medications. She has learned which activities help her stop spiraling downward. Usually hanging out in nature, with kids or with animals helps stop the negative thoughts and feelings of hopelessness that can lead to depressive episodes.

—

A few years after Ali and David moved to the ranch, they decided to open it up to the public. They both missed teaching and knew there was a need for kids and families to learn about the food they eat, as well as how to play outside without fear.

They created their non-profit 501(c)(3) working ranch and nature center with the mission to reconnect people with the outdoors and Ali became a certified ecotherapist.

Golden Rainbow Ranch, about one hour north of Tampa, now hosts school field trips, offers courses for kids, and welcomes families for visits. According to its website, the ranch "especially cater[s] to people with special needs, who benefit tremendously from animal interaction and the relaxation of being in the country."

—

Ali and I walk around her property. We stop at a huge tree. "This live oak is 350 years old," Ali explains as I admire it. "It's older than this country. We call it the Tree of Life. This tree is what called us to move here when we first came down the driveway. We didn't really want 10 acres when we moved out here. Five would have been enough, but when we saw that tree..." she trails off, marveling at it.

"We've done so many activities [involving] this tree," Ali continues. "Being here is just so calming; the tree is the center of the calm."

Then, Ali looks down and starts searching the ground.
"What are you looking for?" I ask.
"A four-leaf clover," she replies. "We'll find one."
Sure enough, she spots one, picks it up, and gives it to me.
"How did that happen?" I ask, shocked.
"It's a genetic mutation," she answers.
"No, I mean, I've never found one before."
She shrugs. "The kids love coming here for that. People will just spend hours looking for clovers."

This ranch does seem magical.

—

As we walk, Ali introduces me to the horse David got when he underwent radiation for his brain tumor. "He was home that year and I was working still because we didn't have any money. I went to work full-time five days a week and he stayed home with a horrible headache. David got this horse and it really kept him going that year. I don't know what would have happened otherwise. That was the worst year. He couldn't even read for a while after radiation. He had to teach himself how to read again, using a different part of his brain," Ali recalls.

Over the course of our tour, Ali introduces me to the shy alpacas; the few chickens that survived a recent massacre from a racoon invasion; Turnip, the companion donkey; and a multitude of other animals roaming around.

Ali describes how she wants to start helping people get service dogs or emotional support animals. "There are a lot of people who need them, but very few people train them," she says.

We meet the goats, some of whom are new. All are still getting used to each other. We even stop to admire a spectacular web a spider had recently woven.

At one point Ali stops and reflects: "I still can't believe I've done this," she says. "I remember when I first started [the non-profit] and needed to make brochures and business cards. It was scary. I never thought I'd be able to handle all the paperwork, or the animals. Growing up, we didn't have warm-blooded animals, just fish and hermit crabs." As we walk up to Peppa the goose, I ask Ali how many animals she has. "I don't know. I think it's about 30 chickens, a turkey, a couple of everything..." she answers.

"This place must make so many people so happy," I say.

"It does," Ali replies. "Even the volunteers. We had to close for a few weeks in February because the flu was going around, and David doesn't have a [functioning] immune system. One of the volunteers is an older woman who lost her wife. She'd been coming here on the recommendation of her therapist and she was telling David that when we were closed, she didn't know what to do with herself. It's become such an important part of her life. We've had people that started off [visiting] as kids and are now volunteers, which is amazing."

—

Much of what Ali has done on the ranch was intended to help David heal, but wound up being just as good for her own healing.

Ali spends her days working on her ranch and hosting courses for homeschooled kids, as well as for others from the community. After years of working with therapists, she's learned many coping skills to deal with her emotions. She's also still takes medication.

"I'm on all the same meds that I've been on for years," she says. "It's a lot of different meds. When I first started, I was just on Prozac, which worked after the first manic episode calmed down. I was on it for a long time and then at some point, I think it was when my dad moved in with us for a while in 2010, it stopped working. They added all this other stuff. I've been trying to go off them, but I can't. It's so disheartening, because I feel like I understand my mind, but I can't always stop the depression spiral without the meds."

Ali's coping strategies seem simple, but simple strategies can often be the most effective. "All I have to do is walk outside," Ali says. "I have my plants and animals. I have my weed books and alpaca training websites. I'm always out identifying new plants and finding new ways to appreciate the animals we rescue. All I have to do is be with nature. That helps a lot."

Ali uses her relationship with plants and animals on her ranch to get herself out of her head. "There's always something funny going on with the animals," she says. "If you're in your head you can be stewing about the past. But if you are in nature, you have to be right there, present, in the moment. It's a distraction from logical, sequential thoughts, but it's also soul healing. It's the right kind of distraction."

"The best part is that there's always something to learn. You go online and there's always a new plant to identify, [for example]. I'm still learning."

Ali has spent a lot of time rewiring the way she works, as she puts it. She worked to readjust the way she looks at life. "Every time I think of something negative, I try to think of something to be grateful for," she says.

She's had to do a lot of readjusting. Her life with David has been full of the unknown. "I'm pretty scared about what's going to happen when David dies. I know everybody will be there for me, but he's my soulmate," she says.

"He's passed out a few times in the pasture. I've gone out there and gotten him. I asked him please not to die," Ali says. "It's weird because it feels like it was meant to be this way. It feels like when I'm in my loving heart I'm not worried about anything, or thinking about David dying, things work out. We get money or volunteers... things just keep showing up at the right time. It's amazing how much worry I've just been able to let go of."

Ali's life is largely settled for now, but she is cautious about planning for the future. I ask about her plans, and whether they include getting new rescue animals or expanding the programs on the ranch. "Everything is up in the air," she says. "There's no plan because of David. In my head, either my dad or David is going to die before me. I have to wait and see how I hold up. I have no idea. My stepdaughter has told me not to worry about the future. I've taken care of her dad for a long time, so she and her husband will take care of me if I need it."

Ali has tried to look at her unplanned future from a positive perspective. "In a way it's exciting," she says. "I'm not worried that I'll be homeless. I'm sort of excited that maybe I'll join the Peace Corps or something. There are a million things that I want to do but I don't know if I'll be able to without David's stabilizing influence. I don't know how long it will take to get back to myself or if I ever will.

There's no way to know that. I'm just doing what I can every day to make it a good day. It'll work out. It has to," she says.

—

A coping skill Ali uses to thrive in her day to day life is to stay connected to other people. "I have a good group of people here that know that I often can't do social things because of David and understand that but are still there for me. I have a girls' weekend coming up. I can only leave for a little while, but I still get to go." Ali's social circle includes a lot of caring women, and a few who also have husbands who are terminally ill.

Ali often praises the outdoors and country living. "I think people are realizing that being in the country is a good way to live. It's so much more natural. Nobody really gets pleasure or peace from looking at square buildings. But when you are surrounded by this much green, it soothes your soul," Ali says.

Amanda Bacon

Of the participants in this book, Amanda is the one who is most recently in recovery. In fact, after our conversation in June 2018, Amanda had to go back to treatment. I wanted to include Amanda's story in this book to illustrate that recovery is not linear. Even if someone has been in recovery for years, they still might need additional help at some point. Asking for help does not mean that you are not thriving or that you are not in recovery anymore. Living in your illness is what is detrimental.

Amanda is a bright light. We talked for hours when we met, and I wanted to keep talking with her. She is sensitive, thoughtful, and caring. Her story is one of great strength and vulnerability.

—

Amanda is originally from the small city of Las Cruces, New Mexico. When we met, she was living with her mother and stepfather there, having recently moved back from Denver, Colorado.

Amanda's parents divorced when she was five and both remarried a year later. She's never gotten along with her stepfather, as he was abusive to both her and her sister. "He was just an angry man," Amanda says. "My stepfather picked on my sister and me." Amanda recalls that he wasn't as hard on her, though, because she was "cute and pretty." "I realized that was keeping me safe in the world. I felt like I had to maintain [my looks]. I could control my weight and that made me feel good," she says.

As a child, Amanda was quiet and followed rules. "I had good friends in middle and high school. I got good grades and did the right thing. People would have had no idea that I had such serious stuff going on at home because I pretended like everything was okay," she says.

Amanda started struggling with depression in 2003 when she was a college student at New Mexico State University. She initially went to school with the intent of becoming a nurse. "But I got nervous, pulled myself back and changed my major," she says. She switched her major to family and child science.

She joined a sorority and enjoyed the experience. "It helped me get my grades up, but I also partied a lot and make some pretty poor choices," Amanda admits.

When she realized she was feeling depressed, she went to see an on-campus therapist. But when she found out that the therapist was a student who would have to record each session, she felt uncomfortable. "I freaked out, so I walked out and didn't go back to therapy again for a while," Amanda says.

Amanda struggled, but graduated college. She decided to take a year to do missionary work in Serbia after graduating. Everything was set; she'd even raised money for her trip. However, she had to get a psychological evaluation before she was able to leave. During her phone interview, she spoke candidly about her eating habits. She admitted that she sometimes purged after eating and that she restricted her food intake. The next day, the evaluator called and told her that she wasn't approved to go on the trip. "I was heartbroken. I was so sad," Amanda says.

—

With no backup plan, Amanda decided to move to Denver in 2007. She had friends in Denver, and she slept on one friend's couch for four months. She still struggled with depression. "I moved with one of my best friends, so I wasn't totally alone," Amanda says.

Amanda got a job at a childcare center; she'd had previous experience in the field. "I worked with little kids. It was okay but I wasn't thrilled about doing it. I wanted to become a therapist so I knew I would have to get a master's degree, but I wasn't quite ready yet," Amanda says.

Having never worked with a therapist, Amanda knew something was wrong, but she didn't know what it was. In hindsight, she recognizes that she was experiencing severe depression. At the time, she says she "felt off, sad, and confused."

She struggled without help until 2009, when she decided to give therapy another shot. She found a therapist she liked but whose office was 45 minutes away. She saw the therapist for nine months, but when her car died, she had no way to get to her appointments and she stopped going to therapy altogether.

While Amanda struggled with depression, she also recognizes that she had attachment issues. "I felt really attached to my friend who I had moved to Denver with. I felt alone and I wanted her to be around me at all times. It made me feel like a freak. I didn't understand why I needed her so badly. She would push me away emotionally, then I'd become more frantic and want to be around her. That was really challenging," Amanda explains.

In 2010, Amanda started seeing a new therapist who helped her identify and give a name to what she was feeling: depression. For the first time, Amanda was prescribed medication. "I didn't want to [take meds] but I also didn't like the way I felt. So, I tried it," she says.

Amanda still struggled. Therapy was helping, but not enough. In 2012, she had her first thoughts of suicide. "Once it popped in my head, I thought, 'why haven't I thought of this the entire time? This is an exit; this is a way out of my pain.' I was hospitalized for the first time because I mentioned these thoughts to my therapist, and she sent me to the psych unit right away. I was terrified," she says.

The next two years were tumultuous, and Amanda says she was hospitalized at least 10 times. "I didn't know how to keep myself safe," she recalls. "No one ever felt like the medications were working correctly. My eating disorder was still very present, but no one really ever called it out. It was just how I ate. Professionals didn't even really call it out for what it was. I just thought it was fine. I didn't call it an eating disorder. I just thought it was normal for me."

The last straw came when Amanda was hospitalized in May 2014. "I was about to be discharged even though I didn't feel like I was ready. I told the staff that I was suicidal. I told them that I didn't feel comfortable with being released," Amanda recalls. However, the staff went ahead with her discharge.

Sometimes, patients get used to going to the psych hospital, and while most wouldn't describe it as fun or a choice, they rely on it and as a result aren't able to recover. Instead, they stay in their illness using the psych hospital as a crutch. This is what the doctors at the hospital were likely considering when they discharged Amanda.

Even though Amanda felt suicidal, she was released. She was infuriated. When a patient leaves a psychiatric hospital, the usual protocol is for staff to wait with them until someone arrives to pick them up. This time, the staff left Amanda alone and told her to wait in the lobby for her friend to arrive. She knew this wasn't the protocol, but "part of me was excited," she explains, "because I was suicidal. I saw this as an opportunity."

She left the hospital without waiting for her friend. "I knew there was a Target across the freeway," Amanda says. "I made a plan to go to Target, buy some pills, and overdose. I walked over the freeway on a bridge. I abandoned my purse and my bag behind a tree because I knew I wouldn't need them because I was dying. I kept my phone and debit card with me," Amanda says.

"I went into Target with my debit card and bought sleeping pills. I don't remember how many, but I bought a lot," she recalls. "I grabbed some water at Starbucks and slammed the pills down in the Target parking lot. I was just planning on walking around until I fell over. I didn't know what to expect."

In the meantime, Amanda's friend, Andrea, was looking for her. Andrea was supposed to pick her up at the hospital. When she realized Amanda wasn't there, she tried calling her. "I waited a while before answering the phone, because I wanted the pills to take effect," Amanda says. She eventually did answer, and Andrea found her. "She asked me what I had done. She knew something was up. At that point I was so loosened up that I told her. I remember her being so calm. She just told me we were going to the hospital to get me checked out," Amanda says.

"We went to the emergency room and we were just sitting there for a bit. Everything seemed fine. The attending doctor told me: 'we are going to be saving your life right now. That's where we're at,'" Amanda says.

"He walked out of the room and the next thing I remember, my heart went ballistic. I've never felt anything like what I felt in my heart. It was beating erratically, and I could barely breathe. That scared me," Amanda says.

Amanda suffered a seizure and a heart attack. She doesn't remember any of it. She spent a week in the intensive care unit (ICU). "It's weird because the last memory I have was of me pulling on my clothes and my heart beating. The next thing I knew, I was waking up in another psych unit more than one week later."

When Amanda was eventually released, she says, "I knew I was lucky to be breathing."

—

The experience was very traumatic for her friend Andrea, and for Amanda's entire group of friends. "I felt so alone. I remember just sitting on my bed thinking about how I had almost died. My friends were mad at me. I didn't blame them, I just didn't know what to do," Amanda says. "I'd also lost my job. I lost my jobs quite a bit because I wouldn't show up for work because I was in the hospital. Of course, my jobs couldn't keep me because I was unreliable. After this episode, I decided to move back to New Mexico."

Amanda's relationship with her mother and stepfather was difficult, and she only stayed in New Mexico for three months. "I didn't want to live in Las Cruces," she says. "It was too small and my relationship with my family can be hard. They love me and I love them, but it's been a very hard environment for me. My family was heartbroken when I left again."

—

Amanda moved back to Denver. She got an apartment

downtown and lived alone. But it wasn't long before she lost yet another job due to her mental illness and had to give up her apartment. "I didn't have savings or anything, so I started living with friends in Denver, all over the city," Amanda says. "I also didn't have a car, so I had to get used to the bus system. I would live with one group of friends or a married couple for a week and I would have to pack up all my stuff and take my suitcase to stay with the other friends. It was really hard. I was grateful to have places to go, but things were really challenging then. My friends eventually got frustrated with me because my behaviors didn't change. I don't think they knew how to handle me. I felt guilty and I felt horrible about who I was. I didn't understand myself."

After six months of couch surfing, Amanda remembered that she'd once heard of a mental health home in Denver called Karis Community. She'd been referred to the home in 2012, but at the time she didn't think she was mentally ill and refused to consider the option. "However, by this point, I was desperate. I was really struggling with my mental health," Amanda says.

She applied and was accepted as a resident of the small community. "I lived there for about two and a half years and it was life changing," Amanda says. "We had groups and therapists on site. We had short check-ins with the therapists but were still required to see a therapist on our own. We were required to work or volunteer because they believed that with mental health issues it's important to have something to do. We paid rent, which was all-inclusive. We had meals together about six times per week. Those were always a struggle for me."

While Amanda's depression lifted significantly in the transitional housing community, she still struggled with food. She took up yoga and started an intense practice.

She got a lot of positive attention for the way she looked. "It made me excited but inside I was like, 'you have no idea what's going on,'" Amanda says. "I also felt sad because people would ask me to give them [weight loss] tips. All I could think was that I was a fraud. I was a phony. I was disgusted with myself. It made me feel really sad that people wanted to be like me."

In 2015, Amanda was diagnosed with bipolar disorder. "I would have a lot of manic episodes. I didn't know what they were," she says. "I just thought, 'this is life, and this is great! I don't have to sleep that much.'"

The staff at the transitional living house noticed that Amanda was not doing well and told her that she needed a higher level of care. They recommended she attend a treatment center. She tried to attend an intensive outpatient program (IOP) in Denver but her insurance refused to pay for it. Eventually, she decided to pay out of pocket but couldn't afford to attend the program long enough to benefit from it.

—

After two and a half years at the transitional living house, Amanda decided to move out. The facility isn't set up for people to live there forever, and Amanda had been there a long time. She and another member of the community moved in together, but the situation turned ugly when her new roommate, a recovering alcoholic, fell off the wagon. She was abusive to Amanda, who eventually left. She moved in with someone she met on craigslist. "She was sweet, but I was just so alone and so confused, and my eating disorder was so bad," Amanda says. "I didn't have a car, so I had to walk a lot and it was really hard. At that point, I decided to move back to New Mexico again."

In March 2017, Amanda moved back home with her parents. It "was not ideal but I was really not doing well," she says. Amanda did not improve at home — in fact, she got worse. Her body was starting to shut down. "I did want help because I couldn't stop [restricting]," Amanda says. "I didn't have a job, so I was on Medicaid, and my therapist and dietician were like, 'this girl needs treatment or she's going to die.'" Still, Medicaid refused to pay for her to attend a treatment center.

"I remember I would journal, and I was just like, 'please God, help me. I don't want to live this way. Help me. I need the help,'" Amanda says. With the assistance of her doctors, Amanda switched her Medicaid provider to one that would allow her to go to a treatment center.

Amanda was eventually sent to Rosewood Ranch in Wickenburg, Arizona. It wasn't easy, though. She had to work hard with hospitals, doctors, and insurance companies to finally be approved to go to an inpatient treatment center. "I felt really blessed and really lucky that it worked out. I went and I struggled, it's hard," she says.

When she arrived at Rosewood, her therapist would only meet with her for 15 minutes at a time because Amanda had such a hard time communicating. "Your brain is not with it," the therapist told her, Amanda recalls.

"I really pushed myself there. I had ups and downs, of course," Amanda says. She spent two months in the inpatient program and then moved to the partial hospitalization program for another two and a half months.

Amanda eventually thrived at the treatment center. Initially, she worked on healing her brain. Once she was able to function better, she started working on recovery.

"I found being around other people who understood to be so helpful," Amanda says. "I had never been around people with eating disorders."

Amanda regained the ability to have complex thoughts. "I could read again, I could write. My journal entries from the first month at Rosewood are very short because I couldn't even do it. I started to feel better and I liked that," Amanda says. "I'd been malnourished for so long that I didn't know I could feel that good."

—

When Amanda and I met, she'd only been back from Rosewood for one month. "It's been up and down since I got home. There are days when I feel like I can do it and I'm doing great. Other days I'm just not okay with it. I'm scared of food and calories."

"A lot of my motivation to recover is that I want to get my master's degree. I really want to pursue nursing. I've thought about being a dietician. It would be really cool to help people with eating disorders," Amanda says. "Before I left, I couldn't pick up my niece or nephews. Now I can do that. I remember that when I got home, my brother's girlfriend had had a baby and I got to meet her, and I could hold her and that made me feel so good. That's been really cool for me. And I've been keeping my goals in mind."

—

On the day we met, Amanda was wearing a pair of earrings she got at Rosewood. Someone had sent earrings to the patients anonymously. She says that when she got home, she found out that a jewelry maker named Amy sent them as part of a small business Joy Over Your Destination (JOY'd). "I wrote Amy and thanked her for the earrings," Amanda says. The two are now friends. "She's really encouraging to me. She's in recovery almost two years and doesn't want to go back. I talk to her a lot."

"I've started caring," Amanda says. "When I got home, I got diagnosed with the precursor to osteoporosis and it made me sad about what I did to myself. But I care. I make sure I'm taking my calcium pills. I'm 34 and I have my whole life ahead of me."

"I look forward to the day where I can go to high school and middle school and talk to [students] about depression and eating disorders," Amanda says. "My eating disorder has kept me safe. My therapist says that I'm scared to move forward and take risks. I don't think she's right, but at the same time, she might be right."

—

Since our interview, Amanda had to go back to treatment. It is not uncommon for people to go to treatment more than once. She spent another few months at Rosewood.

Upon her return from treatment, she underwent a medical procedure to have polyps removed, and they turned out to be cancerous. She is now living in Denver again seeking medical care for her cancer. She's had to undergo four rounds of chemotherapy and has had 30 percent of her liver removed. She is currently recovering from the surgery and will have to undergo another eight rounds of chemotherapy over the next few months. While this is a huge setback, Amanda is working hard on healing.

Caitlin Leigh

Caitlin and I didn't know each other before I started working on this book. We met through an online outreach I did to recruit participants. Her positivity and light immediately shined through during our initial phone call. I couldn't wait to meet her. In the short time I've known her, I've grown to consider her a friend.

Caitlin was preparing to publish her second book of poetry when we met. I purchased her first book to get an idea of who she was, and I immediately related to her poetry. Her poems are succinct and poignant. I'm usually quick to dismiss poetry as an entire genre as it usually goes over my head, but Caitlin's poems are lovely. She has now published three books: Just Passing Through, Hollow Bone, and Breath of Water. She also sells her paintings on Etsy.

I met up with Caitlin while she was traveling to Denver to visit friends in 2018. She'd been living in Seattle but had just broken up with her partner, and as a result her life was in the midst of change. She'd decided to work as a traveling dog sitter for a while so she could roam around the country. We spent the afternoon chatting, me with my usual predictable drip coffee and her with an exotic fruit smoothie infused with tea. She was friendly, animated, and brutally honest about her life struggles.

—

"I feel like I had a really good upbringing for the most part," Caitlin starts. "I grew up in Arizona, in Phoenix. My sister, Lauren, is three years older than me. She's been my best friend since I was a little kid. I was always obsessed with my sister."

Caitlin considered herself a happy-go-lucky kid. "My parents were married, and we had pretty much everything going for us externally. We had everything that we ever needed on a basic level," she says.

She was a very energetic child so to tire her out, Caitlin's parents signed her up for a lot of different sports. At one point she was participating in five different sports. "It was great because I'd just be exhausted," Caitlin recalls. "Sports were the only thing that could keep me focused."

While she remembers her childhood as mostly happy, Caitlin's parents divorced when she was 7 years old. "I think a lot of kids are upset when their parents get divorced, but I remember not being as upset as I should be," Caitlin says. "I remember [thinking], 'this feels right.' Their relationship wasn't healthy. They were fighting all the time. When my mom decided to leave with us, I thought, 'I'm glad this is happening,' because it wasn't healthy at all."

After the split, Caitlin's mother took her and Lauren first to live with their grandmother, and then with their aunt in an apartment in downtown Phoenix. "My mom had to drive us all the way across town to get to school. It was crazy," Caitlin says. "We finally got an apartment with [my mom's] boyfriend who is now her husband of almost 20 years, which is amazing."

The girls lived with their mother but spent a couple of nights a week at their father's house. "He was angry. He hated my mom," Caitlin says. "Usually we'd talk on the phone with him before we went over, and I'd try to get a feel for him to see if he was in a good or bad mood. If he was in a good mood, he'd buy us things. If he was in a bad mood, he'd scream at me the entire time." Still, Caitlin believes her father was a good dad. "I just think he was processing his stuff, but I was terrified."

Caitlin's mom was the one to ask for a divorce. Her dad

thought everything was normal in the marriage. "I think his parents were similar," she says. "[He thought that] when you are married, you stay together, the husband goes to work, the mom stays at home and serves." But Caitlin's mom wanted a career of her own. "They were completely different," Caitlin says. "I'm a lot like my mom so when they split, I think his anger was directed towards me."

When Caitlin started puberty, her personality changed. As a child she was a carefree tomboy. "I was a freaking awesome kid," Caitlin says. "I loved everyone and made friends with everyone, although I had very little attention span unless I was engaged in something active." When she was around 12 or 13 years old, she started to care her looks. She was plagued with insecurity. She'd always been extremely sensitive but now she spent a lot of time worrying about how everyone around her was feeling. "I didn't want to hurt anyone," Caitlin says. "That's when I also began my behaviors with [my] eating disorder. I can't think of what triggered that other than puberty."

As Caitlin's obsession with her looks intensified, she restricted her food, over-exercised, and plastered her bedroom walls with magazine cutouts of famous models. As is often the case, she started getting compliments when she lost weight. "It was exactly what I wanted to hear," Caitlin says. She would spend hours by herself in her room. Caitlin has always loved being alone, but she knows she's better when she's around other people. "I just put everything in a cave and just hung out in the cave until my mom threatened me. She said she would take me to a treatment center."

Caitlin's mother had grown worried about her daughter's behavior even though Caitlin tried to reassure her that she was fine. Eventually Caitlin's mother took her to therapy. She was in the eighth grade and she was prescribed medication. "I was terrified to go on medication because I didn't want to gain weight," Caitlin says. "I was given an antidepressant and things started to get better. I became healthier and I wasn't so fixated on [my looks], but [my obsessive thoughts were] still there. It was like putting a Band-Aid on something."

In high school, Caitlin's behaviors mostly improved, but during her senior year, she developed bulimia. "I felt like everything was out of control[4], but I could control [my food]," Caitlin says. At the time, Caitlin had focused her athletic activity exclusively on tennis. She was a serious player but she noticed that her eating disordered behaviors affected her performance on the court. However, she still signed with Colorado State University on a full tennis scholarship.

—

Caitlin always struggled with setting boundaries. As soon as she was off on her own in college, she didn't know how to say no to people. Early in her freshman year, Caitlin started drinking. "A lot of people can drink, and they are fine, but for me I'm done. I black out and I cry, and people never know what to expect from me," Caitlin says. "I was struggling to fit in, so I drank with my teammates. I developed a binge drinking habit where I would drink heavily on purpose and black out, most times, while also being on antidepressants."

During her sophomore year, Caitlin was put on a different antidepressant.[5] While on this new antidepressant, Caitlin attempted suicide twice in the span of four months.

4   Caitlin's life was not out of control, however, she felt that it was.
5   It is very common that a medication that works for someone for years eventually stops being helpful. At that point, patients need to work with their doctors to help them find a new medicine. The process can be lengthy and difficult.

Eventually, she was put on yet another medication that initially helped. She stopped drinking, but that only lasted a few months.

The next few months were rocky with Caitlin drinking again. She started mixing alcohol with anxiety medication that she used recreationally.

One night, Caitlin was raped while she was high and drunk. She had planned to wait to lose her virginity until she found the one.

"I drank too much to have control over my body. I said no, but no did not stop anything from happening," Caitlin says. "The next day I could not get out of bed. I was so depressed and angry with myself. I couldn't believe what I had done, and what I allowed to happen,[6]" she recalls.

Eventually, Caitlin started seeing a therapist. Unfortunately, it didn't help. She continued to abuse alcohol and pills and engage in her eating disordered behaviors throughout the rest of her college career. She just learned to hide her behaviors from others.

—

One week after Caitlin's graduation, her sister's boyfriend committed suicide. In an attempt to be a source of support for her sister, Lauren, Caitlin moved to North Carolina, where she was working on getting her PhD. "I was just the worst sister ever, I felt," she says. "I was drinking all the time and she was drinking too," Caitlin says. "I wish I could have been a better sister to her during that time, but I think I was still absorbed in my own stuff."

---

6   Rape is never the victim's fault, although survivors often experience self-blame. https://www.samuelmerritt.edu/sexual_violence/fault

After seven months, Caitlin moved back to Arizona and got a job as a behavioral coach. For the first six months, she was doing okay. She had stopped taking her antidepressants and wasn't drinking much, but she eventually fell back into her self-destructive ways.

She started dating a drug dealer, which only exacerbated her addiction. The two dated for three years but she wasn't in love. "I met her, and I knew she was in love with me and I loved her attention. She's a really good person," Caitlin says. "She had all the prescriptions that I wanted. I think she enabled me, and that is not her fault. I was so out of control and she didn't want to say no to me. I didn't want to be with her, but I needed the drugs."

In 2013, Caitlin decided to apply for the Peace Corps. "I had wanted to join the Peace Corps since I was in high school. So, I applied," Caitlin says. The Peace Corps knew about her history with depression and her eating disorder, although she does acknowledge she may have downplayed it. "I was so terrified that they wouldn't accept me. I should have told them, though," Caitlin says. "I wanted to go away, I wanted to serve, I wanted to give back and feel purposeful."

"When I entered the Peace Corps, [I was sent to] Macedonia. I felt free, lost, and alone. I was away from the drugs, the eating disorder, and being dependent on my family," Caitlin says. For the first couple of months, Caitlin felt like she was on vacation. But that feeling soon faded. "Wherever you go, you take yourself with you, and I took an angry eating disorder with me," Caitlin says. She quickly went back to her reclusive behavior from childhood. "I didn't go out; I didn't want to be around people. This was in a third-world country, so it was super isolating," Caitlin says.

STORIES OF HEALING FROM MENTAL ILLNESS   67

Once again, her eating disordered behaviors surfaced. "At that point I felt horrible about myself," Caitlin says. "I knew I was at the bottom. I was supposed to be serving people and I was relapsing."

Caitlin told her doctor in Macedonia about her relapse. After meeting with a Peace Corps therapist, Caitlin was sent back stateside. Initially she thought she was just going home for a month, but she ended up staying permanently.

Caitlin was sent to go to a treatment center. She went to Rosewood Ranch in Wickenburg, Arizona. After a couple of weeks in treatment, she was told that she wouldn't be allowed to go back to the Peace Corps. She was devastated. "Looking back on it, I'm kind of grateful I didn't go back into it because I feel like I would have had a huge relapse. I needed the support," Caitlin says.

—

Caitlin spent two months in the Arizona treatment center, and then spent another three months in California in a less intense program. "This was the start of a new life, an unraveling of deep and painful memories, an opening of the heart," Caitlin says.

In treatment, Caitlin was able to confront her father. "I was really resentful and angry at him," she says. "I told him things he'd done to hurt me, and I don't think he'd realized it. I said the things I never thought I could." Since then, her relationship with her father has improved. "I've accepted it. This is who he is, and I think he's accepted me for who I am."

When she left treatment, one of her best friends from college committed suicide. On top of that, another good friend from high school had also recently committed suicide. "It brought back memories of my attempts, and I wondered why I was still fortunate enough to be alive," Caitlin says. "This still weighs heavy on my heart. I think every person in my life that has committed suicide are like these huge bright lights, they are so sweet and just can't handle the world."

—

In 2015, realizing that she needed a new life plan, Caitlin started focusing on herself. "I started doing self-care energy healing classes. I started taking classes with VortexHealing[7]." Caitlin describes VortexHealing as similar to Reiki[8] but more intense.

"I have been focused on healing and being more loving and compassionate towards myself and others," Caitlin says. "I have experienced hate so deeply that it has been a process, a gentle unfolding of a deep, compassionate love. I am fortunate to be alive, and I have dedicated my life to love, although I am still very much learning."

"I saw myself as a really colorful rainbow, [a] vibrant person as a kid, and going through the mental health issues, I was this big blob of darkness," Caitlin says. "Coming back out of it, my life is full of color and all this poetry and painting. I never saw myself as a creative person ever in my entire life until I went to treatment."

—

7   "The philosophy of VortexHealing is that all of life is One (One Source, One Consciousness, One Divinity), expressing Itself as this amazing experience of creation." https://vortexhealing.org/
8   Reiki is a Japanese technique for stress reduction and relaxation that also promotes healing. It is administered by "laying on hands" and is based on the idea that an unseen "life force energy" flows through us and is what causes us to be alive. https://www.reiki.org/faq/whatisreiki.html

Caitlin started dating Cody, a friend from high school. "I was confused because I like women and thought I'd never date a man, but we hit it off and started dating. He's my first serious relationship with a man," Caitlin says.

When their relationship started, she was still new in her recovery, though. She moved to Seattle to be with Cody. "In hindsight, if we did it again, we wouldn't have started a relationship so quickly after my treatment," she says. "I put everything on him as far as my support system, especially since I didn't know anyone out in Seattle."

Recovery has had many ups and downs for Caitlin, as it does for everyone. "I always struggled with self-worth and I feel like I've just given [my self-worth] to other people, like, 'here, I'll give it to you, and you define it.' But now I'm like, 'no.' I can love myself, it's not up to someone else to define. I know I am worthy, and I don't need to settle for anything less than I deserve."

Caitlin hasn't been on any antidepressants in years. "I'm into alternative healing modalities, so it's like, I'm going to try all of those things before I go on medication," she says. "I know so many people that are on meds and it works for them for a while but then they have to go to something else. There are other things that I can try. I'm going to use all my resources before I have to go to that."

—

Caitlin has developed some strong coping skills. "Coming to Denver for a vacation after [my breakup with Cody] has been helpful," she says. "Usually I'd just isolate and hibernate like the world's ending. I would be by myself and try to process it. But I'm doing the opposite of what I would normally do. I'm reaching out to my friends and support is a huge thing."

"I wanted to spend time with family and friends this year," Caitlin says. "I don't have the job that I want," she explains. "Right now, I need to be around friends and family."

Caitlin is a big proponent of self-care. "My self-care didn't drop when [the breakup] happened. I'm still doing my yoga and my meditation every day and I'm getting a little bit of exercise."

Another coping skill Caitlin uses is spending time outdoors. "Getting outdoors in nature is huge for me. I don't need to exercise, I need to be outside hugging trees and being in the water," she says.

"I'm making myself a priority," Caitlin explains. "I've never made myself a priority. I feel like I have been pretty selfish in my life but now I'm being selfish in a very positive way. I look at being selfish in a completely different way."

Dan Ventura

Dan has asked to remain anonymous. His name and a few identifying details about him have been changed for his privacy.

—

Dan and I worked together a few years ago. He is extremely smart and always open to learn from others. For this interview, Dan and I met for dinner, and after spending some time catching up he told me his story. He is someone whose confident appearance tricks you into thinking he's never had many problems. However, he has always been a deep thinker and because of this, I was not surprised to learn that he sometimes gets entangled in a web of existential worries.

—

Dan is Eastern European, living in California. He is in his mid-thirties and has struggled with depression, obsessive-compulsive disorder (OCD), and anxiety.

While he was never officially diagnosed with depression, Dan believes that it's been present in his life for a while. He first noticed that he was feeling depressed in 2008 when he was 24 years old. He had been living in California but had to return to Eastern Europe after his work visa expired. Dan describes Eastern Europe in the winter as bleak in and of itself, but he was there alone, without a job, amid the crash of the world economy. "Winters in Eastern Europe are not easy on the eyes. It's very grey. It has that whole communist vibe," Dan says. "I joke about it a lot because I grew up there. It's fine generally but in the winter, it can be depressing. Especially if you are not used to it, after living in the United States"

During that winter and the following spring, Dan was in

a deep depression. His family had all moved out of the country. His parents were working at an embassy in another country and his brother was in California. He lived in his parents' apartment alone and had a lot of time on his hands.

Watching the world economy collapse triggered a journey in existential thinking for Dan. "Up until that point in my life, I hadn't really thought on a deep level about certain things like death," Dan says. "It all hit me then. Everything around me and inside me was sad." He began overthinking everything, which only caused him to become more depressed. "I didn't have any tools to know how to deal with it. I was just thinking, thinking, thinking," Dan says.

Dan also discovered a love for coffee. "I was living in my parents' apartment with this amazing coffee machine and they had really good coffee beans. I started making myself coffee. I'd have one in the morning and then another one and another one. I was having two, three, four a day and it really wired me," Dan explains.

"In the middle of my existential crisis, I started to think about the rest of the world and how everything is going to shit," Dan says. "That winter, there was a big problem in Eastern Europe because the heat was provided by Russian gas and Putin was threatening to cut off the gas supply for a few countries. We would have literally died. That and a couple of other things got me thinking and I started reading and learning about the environment and energy resources."

Up until that point, Dan had never sought help for his depression or obsessive thoughts. "Even though I pretty directly described what was going on to friends and family on the phone, the culture in [Eastern Europe] about those types of struggles is much more heavily stigmatized than here," Dan explains. "It's better now here [in California] but in [Eastern Europe], you are basically weak or a lost cause. You are crazy if you go and get yourself evaluated. So, everyone was like, 'nah, it's fine. You're just in a funk.'"

Friends and family advised Dan that if he smiled more, he'd feel better. "I know now that those things are well-meant, but they can backfire. They don't necessarily help," Dan says.

Dan thought that perhaps he was just going through a rite of passage of sorts. "This is something everybody goes through. Just roll with it," he tried to tell himself, "it will pass."

"But it did not pass," he says. He even followed his friends' and family's advice to smile or go for a run, but nothing helped.

—

Looking back, Dan can identify that he was already displaying signs of OCD. OCD often presents itself as patterns or behaviors that people need to perform multiple times. Dan's OCD symptoms presented in his thinking patterns. "I could not stop thinking about a few things, including death and the origin of the universe. Some things that are impossible to explain," Dan says. "My brain was fascinated and disturbed at the same time. It was literally on repeat like a broken record. That's what it felt like."

While his obsessions were growing out of his control, he was also still severely depressed. He spent days unable to leave his apartment, or even to get out of bed.

However, before his depression set in, Dan had applied

to graduate school back in the United States. He began receiving acceptance letters in the spring of 2009. The prospect of a new chapter in his life helped lift Dan out of his depression. "It was a way to get back to the United States and it was an adventure," he recalls.

Around the same time, Dan decided to travel to Istanbul to visit a couple of friends from college. He hadn't ever been to Turkey, and the experience of going somewhere new also helped alleviate his depression to some degree. What helped him even more, though, was that both of his friends had personal experience with depression. "They were the first people that I could discuss these things that were bothering me, and they could understand," Dan says. "They had been there, and they recognized the symptoms. Feeling understood for the first time, I started feeling a little bit better."

He spent three weeks in Istanbul with his friends and it was the first time he realized that his depression wasn't permanently attached to him. "I had lived with the idea that this was never going to go away. This was a permanent thing that had descended on me or something broke in my brain or something went terribly wrong," Dan says. "In Istanbul I was like, 'hey, it's been a few days and I haven't thought about this. So, it's possible that it's not constantly on my mind 24/7.' That was the first time that I got an internal wave of confidence that even if it's there, it doesn't have to be super on and active all the time. Maybe I'm not broken or permanently damaged."

Dan continued to struggle with depression until late 2010, but on a much milder level after the first six months. "I went back to being high functioning/normal functioning. I went to graduate school. I was pretty much totally fine in that school," Dan says. "I was in grad school from 2010 to 2012."

When Dan graduated, he started working for a company that was aligned with his values in a position that challenged him. For the most part, he was fine for the next five years.

"Life was good. From time to time some of those existential thoughts would come to mind or I would remember how shitty life was in the dark period," Dan says. "I would be like, 'yeah, I conquered that. It was just a phase. My family was right. I just outgrew it. I no longer think that.' After seeing a therapist, I know that even if you [think you are] completely done with it, you can always come back with the exact same thing again. And with the same full force. I was engaged with life and distracted enough that whenever I had those thoughts, they were small, and I wasn't obsessing, and it didn't bring me down. I thought I was good."

However, in 2016, Dan started struggling with depression and obsessive thoughts again. "I was sliding into depression and started getting obsessive without realizing that it was obsession yet," he says.

This time, his thoughts had him researching health issues. He was in his early thirties and hadn't spent much time focusing on his health, mainly because he had always been in overall good health. "I had terrible skin, adult acne, who knows about some kind of inflammation happening within me? I drank quite a bit in my twenties, I ate everything, all the fat and the meat and the dairy and all that you can imagine. I became super self-conscious all of a sudden," Dan says.

"I could not stop talking about certain health-related diseases, just pure fear from all my research, late night research, watching YouTube videos, reading," Dan says. "I was getting more and more obsessive and there was a lot of anxiety that accompanied that." Dan found it hard to focus on anything. "I didn't recognize the repetitive pattern, which is crazy when I look back at it," Dan says. "I was so consumed by the actual thought that I didn't notice I was obsessive."

He also grew unsatisfied at work. "It was repetitive to me. I was wondering if we were true to our mission," he says. "By that point I had started to see some cracks in the company. I felt like my team was sacrificing quality and we weren't delivering our best work because of certain office politics and complex client relationships. I grew resentful of those dynamics, which in turn made me jaded and dissatisfied."

Dan also realized his circle of friends was almost nonexistent. He'd spent so much time working that he didn't have much of a social life. He also spent a lot of time alone, which caused him to slip back into his existential thinking. "That's one common theme. All of my depression happened when I was spending extended periods of time by myself," he says.

Dan panicked when he noticed his depression return. "I was like, 'oh shit, this is back. I didn't really win like I'd thought before.' I got really freaked out. I think it was a mix between depression and anxiety," Dan says. He thought he was supposed to be over his struggles. "The depression was back, and I was angry with myself because I couldn't overcome it," he says.

Dan's obsessive thoughts had him researching different health issues, self-diagnosing, and eventually getting a checkup from the doctor with a clean bill of health. He repeated the cycle over and over with different symptoms and illnesses. He became vegan, and quit alcohol and coffee.

"The research from the positive psychology movement was the idea that your thoughts become a reality," Dan says. "This is a terrible thing to say to a depressed or anxious person. They can take it literally, which I did at the beginning. I was like, 'I'm thinking about cancer so I'm probably bringing it on to myself even if I don't have it,'" Dan says. "It made my obsession even [greater] because I was like: 'you can't think about it,' but then I was thinking about it and it only made things worse," Dan says.

—

A good friend of Dan's noticed he was in trouble and suggested he get help, but Dan didn't listen. "It started to get worse. I could not focus on anything else, from the moment I woke up... I was more or less coherent, but I could only do one to two hours of work a day, at most," Dan says. "My OCD was a little alleviated at night... I would do my work at night. At work, I would sit there doing nothing or Googling stuff. I would go on long walks. I had some coworkers that would walk with me. I would literally work from 7 to 9 pm, go home, and go straight to bed. All the time before 7 pm was bad. Most of the day, especially the morning up until the late afternoon, I literally felt like I was on repeat. I could not shake it. I've never experienced anything like that."

Dan finally looked for help. "My friends, family, and workmates were like: 'dude, you cannot shut up about this, you are really bothered, sounds like you could benefit from talking to someone.' So, I did and that's when I was diagnosed with OCD."

"January to March of 2018 was complete torture," Dan says. "I was unproductive. I even took some time off from work. I felt like a completely broken man. Thank God there were some friends that were really helpful and did not judge me. Then in April I went to an OCD expert. She was great. She helped me find some tools that were helpful. I started going at least twice a week and then once a week. It was super helpful. In June, I stopped going because I felt like it was subsiding."

"I was able to focus again," Dan says. "I was making peace with it because of some of the things [my therapist] taught me, like [the exposure therapy]."[9] Dan's therapist told him that he could think his obsessive thoughts as often as he wanted. In order to help calm the obsessions, he needed to refrain from reacting to the thoughts. "If you are not reacting to it, if you aren't resisting it, scared of it, or whatever, it will end on its own," Dan explains. "The brain will only repeat things that need attention. It you tell yourself that you are just going to ignore it, gradually, it will go away."

Dan explains further: "If I say to you, 'don't think about a pink elephant,' you are now thinking about a pink elephant. Saying you aren't going to think about cancer doesn't work. You are going to think about it — that's exposure. Acceptance is a similar thing. Just accept whatever it is. Convince yourself to accept it."

Dan still struggles with obsessive thinking. "Over the past couple of months, it has reappeared, but I've been able to use the tools," he says. "I feel focused and smart again. I've been feeling okay."

—

"When I got back to my apartment after traveling and doing well in June, I laid down in my bed where all the

9   Exposure therapy is a psychological treatment that was developed to help people confront their fears. https://www.apa.org/ptsd-guideline/patients-and-families/exposure-therapy

obsession happened," Dan says. "I looked at the heating vent as usual and I kind of triggered myself. I woke up the next morning and the dark cloud was coming back. I was like, 'oh great, here we go again. I'm only okay if I'm around a lot of people or in a new place. I have to be distracted a lot.' But then, I was like, 'let's apply the tools.'" He did and they worked.

Dan's tools are simple, but effective. "First of all, I can still try to make my days more interesting and entertaining," he says. "I spend too much time alone and working anyway. I'm kind of an all work and no play boring Jack. More importantly, I think, 'let's apply the tools from the therapist: acceptance and exposure and just being calm with it.' I breathe through my reaction to make it physical."

"Now I know not to freak out," Dan says. "Just stick with it and accept what is happening to you, even if it's terrible."

Dan's therapist also had him work on committing to his values. "She had me do this exercise where I had to go through several rounds of going through all my values," he says. "At first it was like 50 things you care about, then you had to pare it down to 20, then to 10, and then to five. So those are the five values that I live for." Dan focuses on "committing to those five things so when the shit descends upon you, try not to give into it, and focus on your values," he says. "Steer your attention to your values. Do whatever it is that you want to do with your life."

"My therapist also discovered that my OCD is a shape-shifter, meaning that my obsession does not stay constant," Dan says. "It wasn't always cancer. That was the looming one for a few months, but gradually it became an obsession about an obsession. Then it was about not being able to focus, and I would fear I wouldn't be able to hold a job and I would be so distracted by the thing that was happening in my head. It's good to recognize the shapeshifting nature of my OCD. It's good to be vigilant about the change that can happen. It's good to recognize the patterns."

Dan has found that distraction works well for him as well. "Going out with people or going to places I've never been helps," he says. "Going to a restaurant that I've never been to before, I'm more likely to be more interested. When I struggle, traveling to new places has worked."

Dan also experimented with nutrition, which was very helpful for him. "I discovered that alcohol makes it worse," he says. "I still drink sometimes but I'm much more strategic on when and how I drink. I make sure the situation is right. Also, different types of alcohol matter for me. Wine is the worst; beer is a little better."

Dan quit coffee in 2017 for a few months. "I took a DNA test and it told me how I reacted to certain things I ate and drank," he says. "Coffee was a big one for me. I never drink coffee at night, in the evening, or afternoon anymore," he says. "Most people metabolize coffee after one to two hours, but I metabolize it between eight to 12 hours. My liver does a poor job of breaking down coffee."

Dan has also started to pay attention to his sleeping habits. "I no longer try to mess with sleep. I try to get at least seven hours. I used to mess with my schedule but it's not a good strategy. I'm trying to work on a consistent bedtime. I'm still working on it. I very rarely go to bed after midnight now," he says.

Being vulnerable and sharing has been helpful for Dan. "I've read a few books by Brené Brown that have really helped me. I share with people that will probably understand. Sharing helps a lot. I'm pretty sure that's universal. There's something magical about knowing that you are not the only one," Dan says.

Slowly, with the help of tips from his doctor, Dan has been able to relieve many of his symptoms. "Things haven't been amazing but [they are] pretty good," he says. "I'm functioning, working, being productive."

—

Dan has recently had to move back to Europe because his green card application was denied. However, he feels he has a solid support system now and is optimistic that the move will go well.

Lauren Marshall

Lauren and I didn't know each other before I started working on this book. We met through an online outreach I did to recruit participants. We met at a local coffee shop in Phoenix, Arizona, in June 2018.

Lauren is a college student at Arizona State University. Not only is Lauren extremely intelligent and hardworking, she is also very friendly and welcoming. While our conversation covered many sad and difficult topics, I enjoyed getting to know her.

—

"I'm from Texas," Lauren begins. "We moved from Victoria, [a town] by the coast, to a small-town north of San Antonio when I was 3." She is currently living in Phoenix while she goes to school. She has one brother who lives in Fort Collins, Colorado.

"I grew up always wanting to be the light in the room, the person that brought everyone up," Lauren says. "If anyone was having a bad day, I just wanted to fix them. So, that was me from a very young age. My mom says I came out that way."

Lauren continues: "I just remember this one memory of being on the playground in kindergarten and people came up to me and they were like, 'Lauren, these two kids are fighting, come help us.' I became the counselor, not only for them but for my family. I think I started to push down a lot of my own emotions. I believed it was okay for them to feel them, but it wasn't okay for me to." Lauren says she was always hyper-aware of how other people were feeling. "I didn't want to hurt anyone."

When Lauren was 8 years old, her parents got divorced. She and her brother lived with their mother. Her father was an alcoholic and would often drive drunk with the kids. "I think his alcoholism is one of the reasons they got divorced, but there were other reasons," she says. "[My parents] just were not compatible. They are both completely stubborn people so they could never come to a compromise on anything. I don't remember any part of my life where they were okay with each other."

Lauren's brother coped with the divorce by getting angry. Lauren, on the other hand, tried to fix everything, true to her personality. Her parents used her as a messenger, asking her to report back between the two of them. She learned to hide her own emotions. "I think that I wanted so bad for everything to be good. I was willing to sacrifice whatever it was. And ultimately, it was my mental health," Lauren says.

When Lauren was in the sixth grade, her father remarried. His new wife was immediately hypercritical of Lauren. "She compared me and my body and my achievements to other kids," Lauren says. She believes her stepmother suffered from an eating disorder. "I think she's still in her eating disorder to this day. She's never had help; she doesn't believe in help. I don't think she realizes that she has an eating disorder at all," Lauren explains.

Lauren's stepmom was always on a diet or cleanse. Lauren realized that she could also control her food and started to struggle with an eating disorder herself. "I got to senior year and I was like, 'I'll show them. I can beat them. I'm going to be skinny and have it all together and have all the control that [my stepmom] is spending her whole life trying to get,'" she says.

Lauren had previously experienced self-defeating thoughts, depression, and suicidal ideation. She thought that she could control her emotions through food. She started to lose weight fast even though never needed to lose weight in the first place. But she received positive feedback from her stepmother and that encouraged her to continue with her self-destructive behavior.

"I got ill pretty fast," Lauren says. "My eating disorder is pretty destructive. I couldn't hide it. It's not one of those ones that you can coast on. I was controlling every single thing I could, and I was so thankful for having this [eating disorder] to distract me from everything."

—

After her high school graduation, Lauren had planned to go on a mission trip over the summer and then head off to Arizona State University for college, but her mom intervened.

Lauren had become so sick that her mom knew she needed to go to a treatment center to get help. At first Lauren refused, but when both of her parents teamed up and told her she couldn't go on the mission trip, she cut a deal with them. "I cried for hours and hours and hours and finally said: 'I'll go on the mission trip and I'll go to treatment when I get back.'" Her parents agreed to the deal.

"I still didn't believe that I had a problem," Lauren says. "I knew I was in some mental turmoil, but I didn't think it was this serious. I went to treatment that summer and still planned to go off to college after."

—

During her first experience in a treatment center, Lauren thrived. "I discovered so much more than I ever thought I would about myself, about other people, about what true empathy is," she says. "Empathy didn't mean that I had to put myself down and sacrifice everything that's good for me. I learned that and learned how to eat again. It was nuts because I'd only had my eating disorder [for a few months]. But I forgot everything about normal eating."

Lauren knew that if she didn't recover over the summer months, she wouldn't be able to go to college in the fall, not only because she wasn't healthy enough, but also because her dad had threatened not to pay for her college unless she was committed to recovery. "College was what I had always wanted. So, I just wanted to beat this thing. Everything was going to be great. I would simply get it over with," she says.

In the fall, Lauren was well enough to go to college. She moved to Phoenix but didn't follow up with her treatment. "The first little bit was fine because I had distractions. I kind of followed my meal plan," she says. But within months, she was struggling again.

Her relationship with her father was rocky because her stepmom had decided that she didn't want Lauren in her life anymore. He was also angry with Lauren because he'd agreed to pay for college for Lauren as long as she followed rules he had outlined: she wasn't allowed to date for a year, she had to go to counseling, and she couldn't let her mother ride in her car (which he'd gifted to Lauren). Lauren's father found out that she'd broken all three of his rules, so he stopped paying and the two stopped talking.

When Lauren went home for Christmas break, a confrontation with her father instigated a relapse in her eating disorder. "I ran full-force back into it," she says. Lauren managed to finish out the school year but went to treatment again over the summer. She spent the summer in Austin, Texas, where she lived with her grandparents and attended treatment at the Eating Recovery Center. "It was really devastating for me because I'd already been to treatment. It was embarrassing. I'd also set up a study abroad in Israel, as I wanted to be a foreign correspondent," she says. But Lauren knew she needed to go to treatment, so she rearranged her summer to go to "eating disorder summer camp," as she calls it.

This time, Lauren spent a lot of time in family counseling with her dad. "None of it made anything better, it actually got worse. I finally realized that our issues have nothing to do with me and him. They were between me and my issues with my stepmom. And his issues were between him and my mom," Lauren says.

Her health was not getting better, and Lauren's insurance company was threatening to stop paying for treatment. The solution was for her to go to a different, more intense treatment center. She was sent to Rosewood Ranch in Wickenburg, Arizona.

"I felt like I was running out of time," Lauren says. "I needed to get back to school after the summer. I went to Rosewood and it changed my life."

—

As part of the treatment program Lauren was enrolled in, she had to cook for herself. Initially she was scared, but she got used to it and eventually thrived. "I spent the summer there recovering," Lauren says. "I really discovered what it looked like to come to terms with the fact that my relationship with my dad may never be how I want it to be."

"For the longest time, I was just redoing the ninth step

from EDA (Eating Disorders Anonymous)[10], which is to make amends. I thought that I could just make amends, and everything would be good," Lauren says. Eventually, though, she realized that sometimes some people are not meant to be in your life. She realized that she was most likely not going to have a relationship with her stepmom for a while.

Since then, Lauren's relationship with her dad has healed, and he helps with her college tuition again. "Our relationship has been so much better for a year now, which is the longest it's ever been good," Lauren says. "I came to the conclusion that everyone in the situation was doing the best that they could. Unfortunately, the best they could wasn't enough to fix it."

—

Lauren has learned to set boundaries with her parents and not to expect more than they can give her. She's told her mom that she doesn't want to hear any badmouthing of her father. "She started to realize how much stuff she had been putting on me," Lauren says.

"For my dad," Lauren says, "I called him all the time and told him how amazing he was. I realized that's what he needed from me."

"I came to realize that I deserve more," Lauren says. "Did I ever think I'd be able to say I deserve anything in my life? No. But thank God I had the ability to go to treatment."

Lauren has been working hard to change her thought patterns. "I used 'catch it, challenge it, change it' a lot," she says. "Anytime I have a negative thought, like, 'my dad doesn't love me,' or 'the reason for my parents' divorce

---

10   Eating Disorders Anonymous is a spinoff of Alcoholics Anonymous

was me,' I realize that I'm thinking that," she explains. "I catch the fact that I had that thought; I then challenge it with things that I know are true. So if my thought is that my dad doesn't love me, I challenge it with, 'well no, he stayed around, he went to all of my functions as a child, he could have just said, 'oh, my wife doesn't like you, goodbye,' and he didn't. The 'change it' is: 'my dad may be disappointed in me from time to time, but I did my best and I know he loves me.'"

Lauren worked hard during her second summer in treatment. After a few weeks in the partial hospitalization program at Rosewood, she went back to school and attended an intensive outpatient program (IOP) in Phoenix. She took a lighter course load than she had originally planned because she had decided to focus on her recovery this time around. "IOP went really well," Lauren recalls. "I think that's when the mundane started to come back. It was in those mundane moments that I was really learning how to be myself each and every day. I would have to wake up and decide to love myself."

"Depression is the one thing that has followed me throughout the whole thing," Lauren says. "I used to not believe in taking meds for mental health, and I thought: why couldn't people just 'get over [their problems]'? But I have a chemical imbalance that has gone through my maternal line and there's nothing that can change that fact."

—

Lauren is looking toward her future. She is still in college and is exploring different career paths. She'd always wanted to be a journalist and she still loves writing. "I had it in my head that I had to be a world-known figure in order to be successful," she says. "Now I feel called to ministry. I don't know what that's going to look like. What I really want to do is tell people about Christ and help people recover." She continues: "I'm doing the things I love right now. I love it so much because I could end up anywhere. I know I'm going to make an impact in some way, just because I recovered."

While Lauren is in recovery, she admits that she still struggles every day. She uses the tools she learned in treatment. "The most helpful thing for me is still the 'catch it, challenge it, change it' skill. I do it and don't even notice it," Lauren says. "I also don't give myself a choice. I play the tape forward. And think, 'if I restrict right now, what is my 'why,' first of all, and second of all, is that going to get me any closer to what I want to do (which is help people recover)?'"

To make sure she stays healthy, Lauren still sees a counselor and dietician. She also attends EDA meetings. "It's really helpful to know that there are regular people out on the street that you could pass, and you'd never know that they have a problem, and that's who I'm meeting with," she says.

Lauren is active on social media, although she acknowledges that it "can either break you down or build you up. It's important to follow the accounts that build you up. Sometimes you have to unfollow people if it's not going to be good for you," she says. "Following body-positive models on Instagram has been really helpful." Lauren uses her Instagram account, @lauren_luvs, to help spread her positive message.

"Talking about my struggles has also been really helpful," Lauren says. Always open about her journey, Lauren has spoken about her experiences at local high schools, at church, and with her friends.

Another coping skill that works for Lauren is having structure in her life. She's learned to pay attention to what works for her.

Lauren knows that even though she still might struggle, her eating disorder doesn't help, it makes things worse. She also doesn't need her eating disorder anymore. She has other coping skills that are much more effective in getting her what she wants.

"What helped me was to stop looking left and right and to really think about what I want to do and what it'll take for me to get there. If I compare myself to someone else, it isn't fair to me because they might be working toward a completely different goal, not only with their body but with their life," Lauren says.

—

Since our interview, Lauren has met the man she is going to marry. The pair met at church and after being friends for around a year, they started dating. They only dated seven months before getting engaged but Lauren says she knew immediately that he was the man she would marry. "He is so supportive of my recovery journey and has seen the growth I've had in just the past year," Lauren says.

Shanda Young

Shanda and I have been friends since high school. When I was a junior in high school, my family moved from Ottawa, Canada, to San Francisco's East Bay Area in California. I met Shanda the following year when I was a senior and she was a junior. We became fast friends. I looked up to Shanda in a way I haven't looked up to many people in my life.

During that first year of our friendship, she came out to me as gay, which was a difficult conversation for her to have. Her bravery inspired me. She was a strong, positive force in my life, and I wanted to be just like her.

While we lost touch in the years after high school, we've recently reconnected and have been enjoying getting to know each other again as adults. I was saddened to hear about how Shanda struggled with mental illness during the time we were apart. Shanda and I met up a few months ago to discuss how she overcame her illness and how she is currently thriving in her life.

—

Looking back, Shanda can see the early warning signs of mental illness in her life. She currently works as a health counselor and recognizes her younger self in a lot of the situations she comes across. "I basically had to create a second persona for myself when I was young. Something that wasn't real," Shanda says. "At some point I lost track of where the lie ended, and the truth began."

Part of this was because she'd been hiding her sexual orientation for years. Shanda knew she was gay since the fifth grade, but she didn't come out until she was a junior in high school.

"In high school, I wanted to pass myself off as the cool

kid, but that's not really who I was," Shanda says. "I was what people that I was hanging out with wanted me to be. I never really felt like I had a solid identity because I didn't feel comfortable with [who I was]."

She initially had trouble coming out. "I wanted people to know [I was gay] without me having to tell them," she says. However, it wasn't long until she started telling everyone. "When I finally did come out, I came out with a vengeance. I was loud and proud. I felt freer than I'd been in a long time," Shanda says. "I used to make up a bunch of stories about how coming out was so hard for me. But it wasn't. It was easy."

Shanda eventually started dating, but her relationships were not healthy. "When I was in my twenties, I dated someone who was very controlling," Shanda recalls. "I didn't really know how to navigate being healthy in a relationship because... when you learn about relationships in high school, it's always between a man and a woman. How do you have a healthy relationship when there's no male in the relationship? I had no idea. I would take on the male or the female role. It would be different each time because I didn't know what I wanted in a relationship."

—

When she was in her mid-twenties, Shanda received a devastating letter revealing a mistake from her past she hadn't realized she'd made. It shook her to her core. "Let me tell you, that was the start of the end right there," Shanda says.

When Shanda received the letter, she had just started a new relationship. "I realized that I didn't know how to be in a relationship," she says. "I kept going back to the letter and rereading it, which didn't help build a healthy relationship. It made me question my ability to do any-thing."

"The situation fed into all my insecurities," Shanda re-members. "I started feeling like I had no control over what was happening. It was four years of self-doubt. Eventually it led to my first breakdown."

While she and her then-girlfriend were on vacation in Eu-rope, Shanda had her first panic attack. "We were in Italy and it was 100 degrees and I thought I couldn't handle the heat," Shanda says. "I thought it was heat stroke."

Her panic attacks kept happening after she got back from Europe. "I felt depressed, couldn't settle down, and my anxiety shot up. I kept hoping there was something physically wrong with me," Shanda says. She went to the doctor and explained her symptoms. The doctor did blood work, but everything came back normal. "That's when I cracked," she says.

"I was sitting at my desk [at work] and I swear I had an out-of-body experience," Shanda explains. "My boss came in and looked at me and asked if I was okay. I just said: 'nope.' We called the mental health access line. I went to the emergency psych unit for an assessment and was prescribed Prozac." Because Shanda thought she was suffering from physical symptoms, she hadn't seen a psy-chiatrist or psychologist.

"I was tired all the time and the Prozac made it worse," she says. "I felt like I couldn't take care of myself. I told everyone that I never wanted to die, but I didn't know how to live. I didn't want to take care of myself. Eventual-ly, my doctor took me off Prozac and put me on Lexapro."

This new medicine helped Shanda get back to being comfortable in her own skin and get back to her life. Unfortunately, her insurance did not cover Lexapro, so her doctor switched her to another medicine, yet again. "When I went on Celexa, it worked well but had a few stronger side effects," she says. "I felt a little down initially but then I started to feel better."

Around the same time, Shanda's girlfriend moved out of the house they shared. "I knew we were having issues," she says, "I thought we were working through them. But she just moved out."

For a while Shanda lived alone, but eventually her sister and her sister's then-boyfriend moved in with her. Things were steady for a while. Shanda had started working with a therapist and was able to go back to work after a six-week break.

—

After about a year, Shanda decided she wanted to taper off her medication. "I decided that I didn't need to be on any medication because 'medicine is for crazy people,'" she says, highlighting a common stigma. She worked with her doctor and started to wean off Celexa.

When she was taking half of her normal dose of Celexa, Shanda and her family went on an annual vacation to her uncle's cabin. While she'd experienced some anxiety on the trip the previous year, she'd had a fairly good time and thought this year's trip would be okay. Unfortunately, the trip brought back a lot of the feelings of depression and anxiety from her past.

When she got home from the trip, she found a leak in her kitchen. "We had to have all these giant fans brought out to dry everything," Shanda says. "The combination of it being one year since my breakdown, the interruption to my routine, and trying to get off the medication created a situation where I felt out of control. I lost it. My mom looked at me in the eyes and said I wasn't there. She said she's never been so scared. She took me to the psych ER again. That's when I was hospitalized for 10 days."

"It was an interesting thing to be hospitalized," Shanda says. "They kept asking if I was suicidal. I said no, I just didn't know how to take care of myself." She was put on a psychiatric hold. "I signed all the forms necessary. I just didn't care. I didn't want to take care of myself."

—

Shanda's family has been very supportive of her over the years. During this hospitalization Shanda remembers that her mom created a schedule for friends and family to visit her. "Someone was there every day," she says. "We would hang out or we would have dinner together."

After almost two weeks in the hospital, Shanda felt better. "They ramped me right back up on my medications," she says. She left the hospital in a better place.

Nearly a year later, Shanda had another breakdown. "I was still taking my meds, but I wasn't sleeping. I was exhausted," Shanda says. "One of my friends was getting married. I couldn't function during her wedding ceremony. I was a bridesmaid and I spent the whole time talking about myself. I wasn't able to be there for my friend and I feel really bad about that. I just couldn't shut up [about my problems]. I feel like I sullied her wedding a little bit and that fed into my negative thoughts about what a horrible person I was."

After the wedding, Shanda's mom stepped in again and

took her back to the ER, where the doctors adjusted her meds yet again. This time she was prescribed the anti-anxiety medicine Remeron, which she took in addition to the Celexa.

—

Shanda was tired of the way she was feeling and the breakdowns she was suffering. She decided to try a different form of therapy called cognitive behavioral therapy (CBT). "I read through Dr. Burns' book Feeling Good: The New Mood Therapy, and I knew CBT was right for me. However, when I would try to work on it myself, I would get frustrated because I couldn't figure it out. I was finding things I wanted to do but not finding ways to do them. Once I found a therapist that was able to help me with CBT, it was an almost immediate improvement," she says.

She stopped seeing her other therapist and focused solely on CBT. Shanda learned new ways of coping with her emotions, one of which she found particularly helpful: "I made a book of cartoons of myself when I'm feeling anxious or sad. I would draw out how I could address that," she says. "It was like doing a thought record; instead of writing it out, I would draw out my record."

"My biggest trap is all-or-nothing thinking," Shanda continues. "I think if I'm not all better, then I'm not better at all. In a thought record, you write down how you're feeling, and then you talk back to the feeling to find a different way of thinking. When I'm feeling down, I just draw [my thought record]."

Shanda has also learned how to communicate her needs. "I can call up a friend and say, 'I'm struggling right now.' I wouldn't do that before. I didn't want to be weak in front of my friends. I wanted to be the strong one," she says.

"There [are] still days that suck," Shanda admits, "but I also find that it's okay to be sad now. You can be sad, you can be upset, you can be angry. For a while I didn't feel any emotions. Now I feel all the emotions. I go through them all."

—

Shanda's relationships with her brother and sister have changed a lot throughout this experience. "I'm the oldest and I was the caregiver," Shanda says. "I was the rock. When I lost it, our dynamic changed. We now lean on each other. I have an incredible support system."

Eventually, Shanda was taken off Remeron. She is still taking Celexa. "I'm about six years out from my last major breakdown and am wicked happy about it," Shanda says. "I was 29 when I had my first major bout with depression, but it had been coming on for years. It took a lot of trial and error, an institution, some meds and good therapy to get me where I am today."

Shanda is pleased to have a job that she likes and finds fulfilling. "I feel like I'm making a difference," she says. "I get to be creative at work. My work has been very supportive. I'm part of a leadership team. I make decent money, but I don't do it for the money."

Shanda hasn't been in a relationship for a few years. "I didn't want to force it," she says. "I might be ready to step back out there. I don't know how to do it anymore [she laughs], but I have a lot of support. I am who I am now. Take it or leave it. I'm not going to change myself. I'm a 38-year-old lady-lovin'-Lego-building-dork who plays Dungeons and Dragons. I'm very creative. I like to write. I like to work with my hands."

"I think I'm a better person to have gone through what I've been through," Shanda reflects. "I've grown a lot. I think there's still the goofy person. But I'm more authentic now."

Nicole Miller

Nicole has asked to remain anonymous. Her name and a few identifying details about her have been changed for her privacy.

—

Nicole and I didn't know each other before I started working on this book. We met online through the outreach I did to recruit participants for the book. I found her story of overcoming her illness inspiring. She and I met in Las Cruces, New Mexico in 2018 where she was studying at New Mexico State University.

—

Nicole first started treatment for her eating disorder when she was 15, but her struggles began when she was much younger. "It's hard to describe," she says. "I just remember telling my mom I didn't want to eat. There was just something weird in my brain. I didn't know what was happening. I just knew that food was not my best friend. I [stopped] eating and developed fears around food."

When she started puberty, Nicole naturally gained a bit of weight. At the same time, her peers started talking about their weight. "I already knew how to control my food in order to not gain weight, so I [did]," Nicole says.

Nicole's parents constantly dieted when she was growing up. Both of her parents were overweight, and they always counted calories. "My mom would always gripe about how I caused her to gain so much weight during pregnancy, she was still trying to lose the weight," Nicole says. "Calorie counting was just normal to me."

"I always thought that being smaller was what everyone

was going for. I thought I should be going for that, too," she explains.

She also notes that every woman on her dad's side of the family has suffered from anorexia. "I am a big believer in the genetic component," she says. "Of course, there are also environmental influences, but if you already have the genetic predisposition, it's huge, you know?"

—

In middle school, Nicole started worrying about body image. She increased the amount she exercised and decreased the amount she ate. Eventually, she stopped working out altogether as she feared she was getting too big. She also stopped eating.

Nicole's parents knew she had a problem but hoped it would pass. "They were hoping it was just my body changing; they were hoping it wasn't as serious as an eating disorder," she says. "They were hoping it was a medical problem and didn't pay attention."

Nicole slept almost all the time. "My head got in the worst state it's ever been in. I would wake up and be so pissed that I woke up. I thought, 'why couldn't I have just died in my sleep?'" she says. "The only reason I didn't kill myself was because I had the possibility of being skinnier. It's like a living hell. I think that so many people with [eating disorders] don't kill themselves because they still have the goal [to be thinner]. There's always a goal. No matter how much your life sucks. No matter how much you hate it day in and day out, there's something to work toward."

Eventually, Nicole's body was starving and rebelled against her mind. She tried to eat again but eating anything caused her significant anxiety. "I told my parents that I couldn't live like that anymore. I didn't know what to do but I was miserable every single second," Nicole says. "They didn't know either. They said they would try to help me eat more and would buy me more food. At that point, I didn't realize how bad it was. I honestly thought I was just dieting. I thought it was no different from the dieting they did, I just did it better."

—

In the summer before her freshman year of high school, Nicole experienced a sexual trauma. "I didn't know how to cope so I took it out on myself," she says. She continued to severely restrict the food she ate. On her sixteenth birthday, she went out to a restaurant to celebrate. "I just said, 'fuck it. I've got to eat something,'" she recalls. "The second my body got food, I couldn't stop eating. Later, I drove to a grocery store and bought all the food I'd ever wanted in the past few years. I just binged on it all that night. In my mind, that was the worst thing I could have done. I went off the deep end mentally and physically. It was the worst week of my life."

Nicole also engaged in self-harming behavior. A friend of hers saw the injuries she'd inflicted on herself and went to talk to their school's counselor. Her classmate also told the counselor that Nicole didn't eat. The counselor called Nicole and her parents in for a meeting and Nicole was immediately sent to a treatment center. "I didn't understand the urgency," she says. "I simply wanted to go back to English class."

Nicole wasn't ready to get help. "I was so deep in my illness at that point," she says. She showed up for treatment but wasn't committed to changing her behaviors. She was initially enrolled in a day program near her home in Arizona, but before long it was clear that she needed a higher level of care.

Finding a treatment center wasn't easy. "There were a lot of places that wouldn't accept me because I had been resistant to treatment," Nicole says. "That made me feel horrible. There were not a lot of people willing to help me. I thought I wasn't worth the help."

Eventually, Nicole was kicked out of the day treatment program since she was so resistant to help. For a while, she wasn't in any program and her health continued to deteriorate. "When you are that bad in your eating disorder, outpatient doesn't really work anyway," Nicole says. "I was just going through the motions in the program, but when I went home [at the end of the day], I was not doing what I was supposed to be doing."

Nicole was finally accepted to Rosewood Ranch in Wickenburg, Arizona. Her eating disorder still controlled her life and she continued to resist treatment. "I played a lot of games at the beginning of my treatment at Rosewood," she says. "I was still in my eating disorder really heavily."

One day, her parents called and told her that they were paying $9,000 a day for her to be in treatment. "They said that I couldn't keep dicking off and wasting everyone's time," she says. "They told me I was getting the highest level of treatment possible. If I couldn't get better in this treatment center, they'd have to send me to a state psych hospital where they'd just give me a feeding tube for the rest of my life. It was eye-opening."

This conversation with her parents changed Nicole's perspective. Instead of trying to be the sickest person in the treatment center, she began noticing some of her peers that were doing well. "They just seemed so much happier," Nicole says. "I thought maybe I did want that. Maybe it would be worth gaining some weight if I could enjoy life again."

That's when Nicole decided to work hard on recovery. "I did really well," she says. "I met my best friend in treatment, we talk every single day. She lives in Arizona, so I go out there a lot and sometimes she comes out here. We really helped each other in recovery."

After spending nearly two months in the treatment center, Nicole went home. She excelled for one week but then relapsed quickly. While she had learned a lot of useful skills, she had a hard time implementing them. Her parents took her to the ER multiple times because she was so dehydrated. She was miserable and she knew her parents had to pay every time she went to the ER. "I felt horrible for that, but I couldn't help it," she says.

—

Eventually Nicole managed to get her act together by using the tools she'd learned. She was a junior in high school and her parents were in the middle of a divorce. "I felt a lot of their problems were my fault. The reason they split up was because my dad cheated on my mom, but I felt like the financial strain didn't help things," Nicole says. "I don't think they were meant for each other in the first place."

Since then, Nicole has suffered through other relapses. "My most recent one was a little over two years ago. We were going on a trip to Hawaii and I was so excited for it. At this point I'd gained some weight and had a new recovery body. All my weight was in my stomach. I was so uncomfortable in my new body. I thought I would just lose a bit of weight before the trip, but it spiraled out of control quickly," Nicole says. "I thought, 'what's my plan in Hawaii? Am I not going to eat? I want to enjoy it.'"

Nicole's main tool for recovery is to stay connected with other people in recovery. "I always thought that I was the exception. I was the person that's not going to recover, and I was going to be miserable [for] the rest of my life," Nicole says. "Connecting with other people in recovery really helped me."

"People who were in recovery and working towards recovery held such a strong motivation to me," Nicole explains. "They seemed so happy in their life. They loved food, and they loved their body. I used to think recovery would mean that I liked every single thing about myself and that life would be great, and I'd never feel guilty about what I ate or how I looked. Now I know that everybody has insecurities about themselves. I've learned that having some body image issues is normal, that it is okay, and I can still love myself. That really helped me. No matter what flaws I see in myself, I know that I still am a person that has tools that can help the world."

—

During her first year of college, Nicole rediscovered her passion for medicine. "I knew if I continued down my eating disordered path, I wouldn't be able to achieve my goals," she says. "I couldn't remember anything I studied. I couldn't learn new things because I was so malnourished. I thought I'd be the world's shittiest doctor. I couldn't stand the thought of hurting somebody else because I was unhealthy. I'd have to be okay with eating enough. That was a really good motivator for me. It still is. Sometimes I think that if I start slipping again, then I'm not going to go to med school and I'm not going to become a doctor."

"I once read in one of Jenni Schaefer's books something that really struck me. She said: 'do you know the weight of Martin Luther King Jr.? Do you know how much Rosa Parks weighed?' I realized that it didn't matter as much as I thought it did," Nicole says. "That really made me think a lot about what my self-worth was."

Now that Nicole is healthy, she enjoys life in a different way than she ever could when she was in her disorder. "My parents and I did not have a good relationship when I was in treatment," she recalls. "They were the bad guys that wanted to feed me. [Eating] was the last thing that I wanted to do. Now we have such a good relationship. My dad and I are super close. It's crazy how much life gets easier if you just eat."

Nicole is still cautious, though. "I think something people with eating disorders have to realize is that they don't get to follow the same rules as everybody else," she explains. "Everyone else might diet once a year for the new year, but if you've had an eating disorder you don't get to follow the same rules. If you are watching all these ads about obesity and if your BMI (body mass index) falls into [a high] category, you don't get to start dieting to change that."

While Nicole considers herself to be recovered, she still sometimes has body image issues. "I don't have any food restrictions or thoughts in my head anymore. Same with self-harm. I think the worst is body image thoughts," Nicole says. "Even those are very few. I kind of just sit myself down and think: 'is this actually happening? Am I actually gaining weight? Am I just imagining this?' And then I go down these routes [in my mind]. If yes, then I think, 'what could it be? Is it something I'm doing differently? Am I stressed out?' If I am gaining weight, usually it's just normal body fluctuations, so I think, 'give yourself a month and you'll be completely fine.'"

—

"There is totally another side out there. It's easy to tell yourself you're the person that can't recover, you're the person that's going to die from this, but that's not true," Nicole says. "It's years and years of tough work and it's really easy to give up. I want people to know that recovery can suck and it's not fun and is really hard. It's a mess to get to where I am right now. I've learned a lot from every relapse and from the whole experience."

"When I first started having eating disordered thinking, I didn't know why," she says. "After treatment, though, I could see that it was a coping mechanism. I could see the correlation."

—

Since Nicole and I met, her life has changed drastically. She decided to quit her pre-med program at New Mexico State University and has enrolled in a new endeavor (which she wishes to keep private). She has rediscovered her love of fitness training and works hard to keep herself healthy, both physically and emotionally.

"I remind myself that life is a journey, not a race. Every experience has taught me countless lessons and I'm blessed to be alive and healthy to experience every twist and turn life gives to me," Nicole says. "My new path will challenge me in ways I can't fathom until I experience them, and I am oh-so-excited to take them on with the healthiest body I've ever had."

Megan Gorman

I've known Megan since before she was born. Our mothers are best friends and my mother is Megan's godmother. We've grown up as part of each other's lives in one way or another. My family moved a lot, so we didn't see each other daily, but we've always been connected.

A few years ago, Megan and I talked about our struggles with mental illness. At that point, I made no secret of my issues, and her mom had told her about my struggles. Megan was experiencing something similar and reached out. I'm so proud of the hard work she's done and couldn't have been happier to celebrate her wedding with her last year.

Megan sometimes gives talks to students about her experiences with mental illness. This story is adapted from the presentation she gives to teenagers and is also based on my interview with her on the day after her wedding in August 2018.

—

"'You're worthless, you're useless, you are nothing without me.' These were the words I was told many years ago by someone who told me he loved me and would soon be my husband," Megan says. "How could I have been so naïve? Why did I believe him?" She goes on to discuss her life leading up to that point.

—

Megan describes her family as "good, educated, and loving." She has three sisters. "I always had someone to play with and talk to," she says. "They have always been there for me and are my best friends. I have loving parents who separated when I was a young child. It wasn't always easy, but I had a good life."

When Megan entered junior high school, things started to go downhill. She was struggling academically and started to hang out with the wrong crowd. Megan says, "I couldn't get a hold of my emotions. I couldn't explain how I felt to anyone because even I didn't understand it."

She started missing school and grew depressed. "Thoughts of suicide crossed my mind and I started harming my-self," she says, "not because I wanted to actually die, but because I was screaming inside for help."

Eventually, Megan was diagnosed with anxiety, depres-sion, obsessive compulsive disorder, and bipolar disor-der. She'd suffered for a long time and saw many different doctors before being able to understand what was going on.

Her doctor prescribed medication to help her balance out, and she learned coping skills. Initially, Megan didn't want to take medication; she thought it was a sign of weakness. She's since learned that getting help isn't a sign of weakness, but rather, "it is a strength, because you are acknowledging you have an issue and are going to do what you can to try and fix it."

Megan started to feel more like herself. "It was still tough, but I started to find myself again," she says. "I had better friends," which she says was helpful.

However, it wasn't long before Megan fell in with the wrong crowd again. To impress these new friends, she started doing drugs and sneaking out her of house at 3 am. She also recalls that she dumbed herself down so her friends would like her.

"I thought if I didn't, I wouldn't be popular and they wouldn't like me," she says. "It is silly to say, but I thought

I would never fall into peer pressure, because my parents taught me better and I was smarter than that. It's so easy to get sucked in no matter what kind of a person you are."

Eventually, Megan was able to find herself again and moved away from unhealthy influences. She wanted to be happy and she knew the only way to be happy was to be herself.

As a child, Megan had been diagnosed with a learning disability; schoolwork was always hard for her. Her high school offered a co-op program in which students would leave the classroom setting and participate in real-life work experiences for high school credit. "It absolutely changed my life," Megan says.

Megan used the hands-on learning experiences to discover what she was good at. She first worked at a museum creating displays. "Seeing what you worked so hard on, on display and everyone complimenting you and praising you, there is nothing more rewarding or confidence-boosting," she says.

She then worked in a bakery, which is where she discovered that she was interested in catering as a career. After high school, Megan went on to college and worked part-time at a catering company. She also worked banquets and events in college.

—

When Megan was in her early twenties, she fell in love. "Things were amazing at first," she recalls. "He had his own car, place, a great job, treated me well. He loved my family. I couldn't believe my good fortune." The pair moved in together after a year and he proposed six months later. That's when things started to change.

Megan noticed that her fiancé's behaviors had become concerning. He wouldn't let her go out alone, gave her a bedtime, made her get out of bed in the morning when he did, and made her sit at the dinner table until she ate all her food. She realizes now that these should have been red flags, but she says she was "too naïve and in love to know better."

Eventually Megan's fiancé's behavior got even more controlling and he started to keep her away from her family. "He brainwashed me to think that they were bad people and that I should stay away from them because he had my best interest [at heart] and knew what was good for me," she says. He would even lock Megan in their room to "teach her a lesson" if she didn't do what he wanted.

The worst came when he threw Megan against a wall and held her by her neck when she didn't obey him. She knows now that she should have left right then, but he had convinced her that she would be nothing without him. "His own sister even warned me about him," she recalls.

—

In 2008, Megan's family surprised her with a trip to California for a family friend's wedding. The trip was two weeks long and Megan's fiancé didn't want to come because he "didn't want any handouts" and he had to work anyway. "He couldn't tell me not to go because he was in front of my family when my mother surprised us at Christmas with the trip tickets," Megan recalls.

The trip was just two months before Megan's wedding date. Her wedding was all planned out and $30,000 had been spent on the affair. "I had my dress, cake, venue, tuxes, flowers, invites," she says. "My mother even hand-made five bridesmaids' dresses and everything was ready to go."

In California, Megan regained a freedom that she hadn't had in years. "I could do what I wanted, say what I wanted, eat what I wanted, hang out with my family. I didn't have a care in the world," she says. "I didn't even miss him, didn't want to talk to him or email him. I felt like a prisoner set free. It was the happiest I had been in years!" The trip changed Megan's outlook on her future.

Upon her return, Megan experienced panic attacks. On one hand, she knew she didn't want to get married, but on the other, so much money had already been spent on the wedding. She thought calling it off would let so many people down. "I remember the loneliest feeling in the world was when I was sitting beside the man I was supposed to be married to in less than a month," she says. "I felt like I was losing control of myself and my life."

Only a few days before the wedding, Megan's mother called her at work and Megan broke down. "My mom asked if it was about my fiancé and I said, 'I don't know, I just don't know what to do anymore.'" When her mother asked if she still wanted to get married, Megan couldn't answer.

With the help of her mother, Megan gained the strength to call off the wedding. She moved back in with her mother and stepfather. "It took me years to get back to the Megan that was lost," she recalls. "I went from being controlled and being told what to do, when to do it, and so many abusive things, to [having] all the freedom in the world."

—

With her newfound freedom, Megan started to lose control of herself. She started drinking a lot and partied a lot. "The wake-up point for me was when I got so drunk, I passed out in the back of a taxi and the taxi driver left me on my lawn," she recalls. "I never wanted to feel like that again. I am better than that."

During this stressful time, Megan started to lose some weight. People started to comment about her weight loss, and before long, she became obsessed. "I was skipping meals, saying I already ate when I hadn't," she says. "It started out as anorexia then quickly became bulimia. I hid it from everyone for years. It was debilitating. I wasn't living a life. It was all I would think about, obsess over, 24/7. Even strangers would comment about my low weight."

Very quickly, Megan became very ill and needed help. "It's the loneliest fight. People want to support and help you but unless you've been through it, you have no idea what it's really like."

Megan knew she needed to get help and she needed to tell her family. "The worst and probably the hardest part was telling my family, especially my mother," she says. "I don't know why, but I was afraid it would hurt her the most or that she would be disappointed in me. I didn't want her to take it personally or think that she failed me somehow."

After telling her family, Megan took time off work and was admitted to a program at her local hospital. While this helped, she continued to suffer with her eating disorder for seven more years. "I realized through my eating disorder program that I was covering up the pain that my ex-fiancé caused me and that was my way of dealing with it," she says.

—

Throughout her struggles, Megan was able to graduate from college with a degree in hospitality and event management. She started a full-time job working events at a convention center and loves it. "Because I didn't give up, I now get to work million-dollar events, with famous people such as Cher, Emma Watson, the Prime Minister, Larry King, and so many others. I also work with a catering company whose chef/owner lets me coordinate and cook for him. I've been in famous and established people's houses," Megan says.

Megan also decided that she wanted to see the world and is proud to have traveled to England, the Dominican Republic, and South Korea. She even went to Peru by herself. "I swam in the Amazon River and climbed Machu Picchu," she says. "I would never have found the courage or have had these experiences if I'd stayed where I was in my previous life."

"My mother always said as I was growing up, 'don't depend on anyone to get you through life. Stand on your own two feet and support yourself because at the end of the day, it's you that you are living for,'" Megan says. "I always have that in the back of my mind in everything I do."

—

Meanwhile, Megan started dating another man. She fell in love again and thought they would get married. But five years into their relationship she still hadn't met his parents. Megan realized that his parents didn't approve of their relationship because he was East Indian and she was Caucasian. She began to doubt herself again. "I started to believe that I wasn't good enough for him. I started to feel bad for who I was. I would start comparing myself to others," Megan says.

During that time, many of her friends were getting married and having kids. This was what Megan wanted for herself. When she realized that her relationship was going nowhere, she ended it. "I had a hard time getting back on my feet," Megan says. "I didn't trust anyone in my future relationships." Megan was also still very sick with her eating disorder at the time.

Around the time of her breakup, Megan was prescribed a new medication. This one helped her feel better and helped curb her unhealthy urges, and she was finally able to recover from her eating disorder.

—

Megan's family has always been a great support system and motivation for her. She has four nieces, one nephew, and one great-nephew. "They are the light of my life," she says. "I want to be a good role model for them. I want to be the best I can be for them no matter what it takes."

One of Megan's sisters encouraged her to try online dating. Megan signed up for eHarmony and after going on a few dates, she met Anthony. "Who knew I would be matched with a male version of myself?" she says. "He is a video game-playing, superhero-loving, movie-watching, UFC and boxing maniac just like me. I could not have handpicked anyone better."

Anthony and Megan fell in love quickly. "We didn't want to be apart and haven't been apart since we met," Megan says. "We are that couple that makes everyone want to vomit because we are so cheesy and in love! I know there is no such thing as perfect, but I feel like we are pretty darn close!"

Still, Megan struggled with trust issues, especially at the

beginning. "It was hard at first because of all that I have been through, but slowly he has shown that he is not like others, and I wholeheartedly trust him," Megan says. "I haven't made it easy on him, but he never gave up and eventually knocked down my protective walls."

"I'm the best I've been, the happiest, healthiest, calmest, and the strongest I've ever been," Megan says. "Anthony makes me feel confident and makes me feel beautiful."

"My motto in life, after everything I've learned through my experiences, is to 'never settle for less than you deserve, because someday you can have it all. Listen to your heart.' If I hadn't listened to my heart, I would be living a life of feeling unfulfilled and empty."

—

Megan never hid her mental illnesses from Anthony. She's been able to talk to him about it and that has been helpful for her. "I never felt judged," she says. She's now able to look forward. "I want a future. I want to have kids. The way I was before, I would have had a tough time having children. I want to be a better person because of him."

Megan still sometimes struggles with anxiety or unhealthy thoughts, but she's now able to remind herself of what's important to her in life. She knows that surrounding herself with other people is good for her. She still stays away from food that might trigger her eating disorder. She has a weakness for peanut butter, so she just doesn't buy it, or she might only buy a small jar.

"A lot of things that helped me were just doing things I love," Megan says. "I love coloring. I will just sit there and color. It's like my Zen."

One of the most important lessons Megan has learned is that you must want to get better. "You can't do it for other people," she advises. "You can't say to someone: 'you have to get better for me.' You have to want it, or it will never work."

Megan has a reason to want to be healthy. She wants a different future than the one an eating disorder can offer. She wants to be happy. "I knew deep down inside that I wasn't meant to marry [my first fiancé]. It was always in the back of my mind," she says.

Megan and Anthony got married on August 4, 2018. She was so calm and happy throughout the entire ceremony. Clearly, she was exactly where she wanted to be.

Brittney Quintana

Brittney and I didn't know each other before I started working on this book. We met through an online outreach I did to recruit participants. We met in her hometown of Fountain Hills, Arizona. Fountain Hills is a small-town east of Phoenix known for hosting a community of snow-birds every winter. When the snowbirds leave, the town shrinks in size and slows down for the summer.

We met at a local restaurant for dinner in June 2018 and she graciously shared her story of recovery with me.

—

B rittney was born in California and moved to Fountain Hills when she was 3 years old. Her parents moved there for work and some of her extended family already lived in town.

Brittney was only 8 years old when she started exhibiting signs of an eating disorder. "My dad's drinking played a large part in it. I think the family dynamic was very chaotic because of that," Brittney says. "I didn't really know what I was doing, but that's how I would cope. It wasn't that I needed to lose weight."

Eating disorders often manifest as a way for people to cope with a difficult situation. When people feel they do not have control of their life, they subconsciously find ways to be in control.

"My parents knew about it and just ignored it. My mom would make comments about it, but it was never handled," Brittney says. "We'd have these crazy Christmas parties and we'd play happy family. For one night I'd choke down some soup."

"When we finally realized that I needed help, I was in

my freshman year [of high school]," Brittney says. She'd started seeing a therapist the year before, but it wasn't helping. She ended up being rushed to the ER as a result of complications from her eating disorder. The doctors said she needed help. "They basically told my mom that she needed to get me [to a treatment center] now," Brittney recalls.

Brittney was sent to Rosewood Ranch in Wickenburg, Arizona. She immediately embraced recovery. "I never ran," she says. "It was my first reality check. There were people I could talk to. Overall, I had a good experience. I also really liked the people who worked there."

Brittney did well for a while after leaving Rosewood. However, before long, she developed a pattern of falling apart, getting help, and getting herself back together, only to fall apart again and repeat the cycle. This pattern affected her ability to stay in school. "School was basically on hold. That was not ideal," Brittney explains. "My junior year, I was in and out of treatment centers, nothing was sticking. Out of the blue, my parents said we were going for a spa day in Sedona, [Arizona]. When I got out of the car, we had pulled up at a boarding school."

The therapeutic boarding school, in Prescott, Arizona, was Brittney's home for the next two years. "Their whole philosophy was to treat the trauma or whatever was causing the eating disorder. It saved my life. I adore that school. I adore my friends. Although, it was rough," she admits.

"It was discouraging to think that there will never be a day when I will be normal," Brittney says. But things improved for her immensely once she started working on the cause of her eating disorder, rather than just the symptoms. "When I started working on what I needed to work on, I got better. It doesn't mean I'm not sad sometimes, but it's fleeting. I get sad, and I recognize that and then I go on with my day," Brittney says.

"[The school was] very on top of all the newest trends with psychology and treatment. We did lots of intensive workshops. They brought in a bunch of different [specialists]," she says. Of all the healing methods offered, Brittney found body work[11] to be the most helpful.

"What actually worked for me was physical work," Brittney says. "I did a lot of talk therapy, but a lot of the issues weren't being physically addressed." She then worked with her therapist using eye movement desensitization and reprocessing (EMDR).[12] After a year, she started doing Tension and Trauma Release Exercises (TRE).[13]

"The idea is that after animals give birth, their body shakes. It's shaking to get rid of the trauma," Britney explains. Dr. Berceli "came up with the idea to transfer that into recovery work itself. You basically do these exercises. You lay on the ground and your body starts vibrating. It sounds creepy but it absolutely works, and I think it if your body has gone through physical trauma, like purging, it can be very helpful. It helped move all that bad energy I had out of my body." Initially, Brittney

---

11   "Body-Centered Psychotherapy describes therapeutic approaches that integrate a client's physical body into the therapy process." http://www.ashleyeder.com/approaches/body-centered-psychotherapy/
12   EMDR is "a psychotherapy that enables people to heal from the symptoms and emotional distress that are the result of disturbing life experiences." https://www.emdr.com/what-is-emdr/
13   TRE is "a simple yet innovative series of exercises that assist the body in releasing deep muscular patterns of stress, tension and trauma. Created by Dr. David Berceli, PhD, TRE safely activates a natural reflex mechanism of shaking or vibrating that releases muscular tension, calming down the nervous system. When this muscular shaking/vibrating mechanism is activated in a safe and controlled environment, the body is encouraged to return back to a state of balance." https://traumaprevention.com/what-is-tre/

was skeptical. "I didn't really believe it at first, but after a few months I could start to tell a difference, even just little things. I would react differently to things than how I used to."

With the help of the therapeutic boarding school, Brittney was able to graduate high school on time. She decided to attend a small college in Kansas. "Going from being in a therapeutic setting to having total freedom was not a good idea," she says. "Things got out of control immediately. I partied a lot. I'd never had a job, I'd never had responsibilities, I'd never paid a bill. I ended up coming home in November and didn't go back."

While in Kansas, Brittney contracted an infection and was prescribed Hydrocodone. She took some time off school and within a month, she broke her leg on a trampoline. At the hospital, she was prescribed Percocet. Shortly thereafter, Brittney had her tonsils removed and was prescribed yet more pain medicine. She was on some type of pain drug for five months; without her realizing it, her body had come to depend on pain killers.

"After I was done with the meds for my tonsils, I stopped taking the pain pills. I didn't think anything of it," she says. "I still had a decent amount left but I stopped taking them. Within a couple of hours, my body was in full withdrawal. It was the worst experience of my life."

Brittney had to detox her body from the meds and was able to do it at home under the supervision of her parents. "No one was prepared for the mental aspect of it," she says. "They were just focused on keeping me safe. I wasn't addicted mentally. I never had the desire to get back on the meds, the pain of the withdrawal wasn't worth [it]. I won't take any pain meds now. I'm even weird about taking Advil."

—

Brittney has developed some long-term medical issues as a result of her eating disorder. She has thyroid issues and her esophagus has been damaged from purging.

She has decided to take life a little slower. She's back in college and is planning to go to grad school when she finishes her undergraduate degree.

Brittney has turned to yoga as a healing method in her life, both mentally and physically. "I had to move my body, even though I was weak," she says. "I like to see what I can do with my body. I can do things that I never thought I'd be able to do. Even when I was in the hospital and just had to stay in bed, I could do bed yoga. It would give me some peace of mind."

Brittney's parents are now divorced but they both still live in Fountain Hills. Her relationship with them has improved immensely. "I didn't talk to my dad for years," she says. "I did a lot of family work. One of the theories at the school was that I could change, but if I went back into the same situation, I would just go back to the same problems I left." The school worked closely with families to prevent this from happening.

"My mom was busy, but she always tried to physically be there," Brittney says. "My dad stepped back a little more, but he's still very much involved in my treatment. They ended up paying for my therapy because it wasn't covered by insurance."

"My mom did everything she could," Brittney says. "Even though she couldn't relate, she [did a lot of research and] knew what she was talking about."

—

Brittney's father has been in recovery from alcoholism for eight years. She knows that his alcoholism was a factor in her parents' divorce. "They became best friends after that. It was better when they were not [married]," Brittney says.

Brittney understands that recovery is not always easy and that she will have slip-ups. "There have been times where I've thought I was going to have to go back to treatment. It has not happened, though," she says. She still has hard and stressful times but has found other ways to deal with things. She proudly tells me that she hasn't relapsed in years. "It'll be four years in February," she says.

Brittney finds value in planning. "I make lists," she says. "I know I can't plan for everything. Instead of saying I'll never do this or that, I try to take things day-by-day. If I mess up one day, or one meal, it's not that bad." She worries about the future and the unknown but has learned that slowing down and not looking too far ahead works to help keep her grounded.

Kylie Dunning

Kylie and I didn't know each other before I started work-
ing on this book. We met through an online outreach I
did to recruit participants. We met at a coffee shop in
New Mexico in 2018. While my impression of her was
that she was very shy, Kylie was thoughtful and honest
about her struggles with mental illness.

—

Kylie was 12 years old when she realized that something was wrong. That was when her parents split
up, although they didn't divorce for another four years.
Kylie's mother was an alcoholic, which often left Kylie in
the position of needing to raise herself. Instead of having
a mother, "it was like I had a roommate," she says.

Around that time, Kylie started to struggle with low
self-esteem. She constantly compared herself to others.
She says that when she was younger she had a pudgy
stomach and people would make comments about it. As a
result, Kylie started restricting what she ate.

"I remember dinner time being a strained time," Kylie recalls. "I used to think I would have to entertain everyone.
There was fighting at the table, so it wasn't fun. We had
healthy home meals, but you just didn't want to be at the
table."

She also felt depressed and had anxiety. Kylie describes
herself as an overall anxious person. Kylie's family history includes depression and possibly eating disorders,
although she isn't sure. "My mom, my aunt, and my
grandma were always dieting and saying they were so fat.
That was a normal thing," she says. "I think my mom has
an eating disorder sometimes."

After six years of struggling, Kylie's parents set up an intervention for her. Kylie did not think she had a problem. She'd heard about anorexia but didn't understand that she suffered from the disease. "When I went to the hospital, I was like, 'you guys are going to feel really stupid because I don't have an eating disorder. I'm going to be out of here in two days,'" Kylie recalls.

Of course, she was suffering from anorexia, and she was admitted to a treatment center. Kylie went to Remuda Ranch in Wickenburg, Arizona. She came to terms with the fact that she did have an eating disorder. Her first experience at Remuda helped, and when she left, she was supposed to attend an intensive outpatient program (IOP). She didn't do it, and within six months she had to go back to Remuda for a second time. She only lasted three weeks there before she threw a fit and left the treatment center.

Kylie managed to get herself healthy without the help of a treatment center and stayed healthy for the next year. Then she experienced the trauma of being sexually assaulted. "I wouldn't eat, I was depressed, I wouldn't get out of bed. That's when I got to my lowest weight," Kylie says. "I remember calling my dad and saying, 'I can't do this anymore. I just want to die.'"

Kylie's dad told her that she needed to go back to treatment, but she refused. He set up her admission to another treatment center anyway. Instead of going back to Remuda Ranch, Kylie was sent to Rosewood Ranch, also in Wickenburg.

Her third experience in a treatment center was the longest. She spent almost three months in the inpatient program and then transferred to the less intensive partial hospitalization program (PHP) at Rosewood called Capri. But she struggled in the PHP.

She hadn't ever cooked for herself, and Capri required each patient to cook their own meals. The staff helped patients cook once a week but otherwise they were on their own. "They accused me of restricting, but I was like, 'I don't know how to cook,'" she says. "I can make a quesadilla and cereal. I was getting frustrated."

Kylie also had a hard time getting along with her therapist at Capri. After less than two weeks, she left against medical advice. When she left, she was told that she'd be back within a year. This lit a fire under her. "I wanted to prove everyone wrong," Kylie says. She worked hard on her recovery and did not go back to treatment. "It still surprises me," Kylie admits. "I don't really follow a meal plan anymore. I feel like I'm a normal person. I'm at a healthy weight."

When Kylie left Capri, her therapist back home said she couldn't treat Kylie because she had left treatment against medical advice. So, Kylie went without a therapist for over a year. Eventually, her therapist did take her back, after it became clear that Kylie had changed.

Kylie's relationship with her parents has improved a lot. "I used to hate my mom," she says. "We had no relationship in high school. We are a lot better now. After family week [in treatment], it was awful, but it helped a lot," she says.

Kylie is now settled in her life. She practices yoga regularly. "It really helps me," she says. "It's not a lot of exercise, but it's still some movement. And it [offers] peace within yourself."

Kylie has a strong group of friends, which she finds very helpful as part of her recovery. She used to hang out with people who were bad influences on her. She smoked weed, binge drank, and took pills recreationally. She would do anything to help herself numb out. Kylie now drinks socially without it being a problem. However, she knows alcoholism runs in her family, so she's careful.

—

She's been working different jobs. She works as a waitress and as a seasonal employee at Target. She's also in school again after taking some time off. Kylie is studying early childhood education and is considering also studying psychology. "I love psychology and thinking about why we do what we do," she says.

Kylie has learned to ask herself what's really going on when she feels triggered by thoughts around her eating disorder. She's also learned to stop comparing herself to others. She says she got tired of it after a while. "It doesn't get you anywhere. Why would you want to be sicker than you already are?" she says.

Kylie has experienced some severe trauma in the past few years. After she was sexually assaulted, she decided to move back home with her mother. "I think I was date raped," she says. "I can't remember a huge block of time and I woke up the next morning to him having sex with me. He left and I didn't remember anything."

Another trauma occurred earlier in 2018. Kylie's sister's boyfriend, Colton, died after he jumped off a dam. "Colton was like my brother; I've known him my whole life. My dad called and said, 'Colton jumped, and we can't find him.' I thought he jumped, got out [of the water] and was somewhere in town. He'd been drinking. We don't know if his friends were fighting and he was pushed in or if he fell by accident, because he jumped in with his boots on," Kylie explains.

The town held a search party to find him. Two days after the incident, Kylie's dad found Colton's body. "He was gone," Kylie recalls. "I feel like I was trying to be strong for [my sister]. I didn't want my sister to see me upset. I was bottling it in."

A third trauma for Kylie took place a few years earlier at one of the treatment centers she was in. She saw a patient die due to her eating disorder. This sad event made her analyze her life. "I knew I was either going to die or get better," she explains. She knew that she didn't want to be sick.

"I was just done. I didn't want to be that sick. It was so much wasted time," Kylie says. "It's so exhausting and miserable to even think about."

—

Kylie is pleased that she can now eat in moderation. "I'll catch myself eating a piece of cake, something I never would have eaten before." She no longer struggles with restricting, although she does admit to struggling with body image sometimes. "I've never been at the weight that I'm at now," she says. "I like it. I wouldn't want to lose weight, but there are days when I look in the mirror and think I look fat."

For almost two years, Kylie has been at a healthy weight and has started to teach herself to cook.

She has stopped seeing a dietician; she no longer needs that type of help. Nor does she follow a meal plan. "I know if I'm in my eating disorder, I need a meal plan, but right now I don't really follow one," Kylie says. "My family was surprised when I gained weight, and people said, 'you look good, you've filled out.' It makes me feel good."

A coping skill that Kylie finds helpful is taking a break from social media. "I find myself comparing. Not just bodies, but lifestyles too. I don't want to live my life like that, though," Kylie says.

Kylie has also picked up hobbies, enjoys yoga, and she's stopped doing drugs. "I used to mostly smoke weed," she says. "It would just depress me and give me anxiety. Before it would numb me, and I had to have it. Sometimes I miss it but then I do it again and I realize it's not like it used to be."

Kylie still drinks alcohol occasionally, but she's learned her limits. "I know I can't drink when I'm going through a depressive episode. I know that if I'm going to drink, I'm going to keep drinking and I'll start crying," she says. "I get super dark, talking about suicide. I don't want to die but I guess drunk me does. I guess I need to talk about that in therapy still."

"I have my wise mind and my eating disordered mind," Kylie says. "I still catch it sometimes and think, 'that's not you, that's your eating disorder trying to manipulate you.'"

"I still suffer with depression and anxiety. I think that's my biggest thing," Kylie says. She thinks the anxiety is a result of the fighting that went on in her house growing up.

—

"You literally can recover," Kylie advises. "It's hard work but you can do it. I've worked my ass off, but I've done it. It's totally worth it. I wish I had realized that earlier. I used to watch people when they would come tell their stories [of recovery at treatment centers]. I thought, 'that would be cool,' but I never thought I'd be that person. It wasn't easy but it was worth it."

Kylie has been thinking of going back to Rosewood Ranch to speak about her experience. "It's going to be different being on the other side... telling people," she says. "But I'm excited for it."

Courtney Pankrat

I am in awe of each person who participated in this project. I know how hard it is to open yourself up to the world and tell your story. I decided to tell my story as the last chapter of this book.

—

I always thought I was a happy kid. I grew up traveling the world with my parents and two sisters. We are Canadian but I grew up in Paris, France, Ottawa, Canada and multiple cities in the United States. I spent most of my childhood in Paris, which offered some amazing opportunities. In many ways I had a very charmed childhood.

I started to notice something was wrong when I was around 11. We had moved from Paris back to my hometown of Ottawa, and it was a difficult time for me. My sisters and I all skipped a grade due to the difference in the education systems.

Academically, I was fine but since my birthday is at the end of the year, I was almost two years younger than all of my classmates. When I was 11, my peers were turning 13 and at that stage in life, those two years make a big difference. I was still playing pretend and riding my bike while my peers were getting bras and kissing boys.

In retrospect, I see that I became highly anxious, but I didn't recognize it at the time. I used to make extremely detailed schedules for myself, including scheduled times to go to the bathroom, brush my teeth, and get dressed. On more than one occasion, I woke up in the middle of the night and, thinking it was morning, started getting ready for school. I have a distinct memory of taking a shower at 2 am, and another of eating cereal in the dark thinking it was just early while it was actually the middle of the night.

I was suffering from a major internal struggle. I thought there was something wrong with who I was at my core. My therapist has since suggested my emotional turmoil started much earlier in my life, and maybe it did. But I remember being 13 years old and thinking that every decision I ever made was wrong.

I was a clumsy, chubby, uncoordinated kid. I was the kid who broke something in every store we ever went to, and as my sister once told me, I always had "sweaty hands." She was right. I did always have sweaty hands because I was always running from one place to another. As I got older, I believed that who I was, on a fundamental level, was just wrong.

I decided that I would become an actress in life. I started to study how to be what I considered "right." I made up strict rules for myself. I had rules that ranged from which foods were okay to eat to what types of emotions I was allowed to feel in reaction to specific situations. However, my basic rule structure didn't make sense. And since these rules were not based on anything real, I had to learn each and every one individually.

My life was tiring, and I'm often reminded of how much cool stuff I could know about the world if I hadn't spent so much time learning made-up rules.

—

When I was 14 years old, my family had moved again, this time from Ottawa to the San Francisco Bay Area. I was entering my junior year of high school and once again I struggled to make friends. I decided that I needed to "grow up," and to me, this meant that I needed to lose weight.

At first, it was easy to restrict the food I was eating. I was so used to following random rules that an eating disorder was a perfect place for my mind to go. I restricted heavily during my senior year of high school and lost some weight.

The next year, I went off to college and decided that I wanted to be a rower. I had never been on a sports team, other than struggling through one season of junior varsity softball in my junior year of high school. Going to college meant that I got to reinvent who I was. I got to decide what kind of person I wanted to be. And I'd decided I wanted to be an athlete.

I spent the next four years of college focusing mostly on my career as a student athlete.

By my sophomore year, my eating disorder had gone from restricting food here and there to bingeing and purging daily. I would over-exercise, which was easily explained as I was a college athlete. I would restrict as often as I could, and when I couldn't, I would force myself to throw up the food I'd eaten, no matter how little food it actually was. I struggled on and off with bulimia throughout college. I saw a nutritionist and therapist occasionally but for the most part, I struggled alone.

During that time, rowing was my life; I lived for it. But once I graduated, I was completely lost. The identity that I had carefully crafted for myself was gone and I had no idea what to do next. Additionally, once I graduated and had no reason to stay healthy for rowing, my bulimia took over.

I had very few friends at the time and eventually lost most the friends I did have. The people I had spent the previous four years with, my teammates, fell out of my life one by one. I can't blame them. I wasn't authentic or

being true to myself. How can you be friends with someone who faked everything in their life? We had no real
connection. However, this confused me at the time. I was
so shut down that I thought that my peers would like me
if I was the best rower. So, I worked very hard to be the
best. I wouldn't say that I was not liked on the team, but
I never figured out how to bond with my teammates in a
meaningful way.

—

In 2001, I was 20 years old, I had a college degree and the
only thing I'd ever been semi-good at (rowing) had ended.
I barely made it into grad school and quickly filled up my
schedule with as many things as I could think of that I felt
would be the "right" thing to do.

I got a job that I could turn into a career. I also helped as
an assistant coach on a rowing team, and I went to grad
school to study sport management.

It wasn't long before I graduated with a master's degree
and focused solely on my job. I was proud of my job as a
manager at a fitness facility. I felt like I was so lucky to
be somewhere where I could grow. I worked more hours
than anyone should; in fact, my bosses used to take me to
the movies or to do activities during the workday in order
to show me that I didn't need to work as much as I did.

—

When I was 24 years old, I decided that my life was almost
"perfect." I was successful at work, and even owned a
home. I had some friends but again, my friendships were
fairly superficial. It was all I could handle. On paper, it
looked like I had life figured out. I decided it was time to
heal from the eating disorder that had plagued me since

high school. I called a therapist who specialized in eating disorders and set up an appointment.

I went to the first appointment to get cured. Initially, I thought that I'd done my part by signing up for therapy. I looked at it like having a broken bone: you go to the doctor, they fix it. Therapy doesn't work like that. Not even a little bit.

My primary care doctor, therapist, and nutritionist formed my treatment team. I initially checked in with each of them around once or twice a month. However, in my zeal to get over my eating disorder, the exact opposite happened. I started using laxatives, I binged and purged constantly, and I worked out at least twice a day, every day. I quickly lost a lot of weight.

People started to notice and complimented me. While I realized that what I was doing was harmful, a huge part of me felt like I had achieved the goal I'd set out to reach. At that time, my goal of being thin was the only thought that consumed me. My years of rules had messed up my head so badly that I honestly thought there was no more depth to my problem than my weight.

—

Therapy was hard. I would sit in the waiting room with some work I'd brought, and I'd run through my work documents in my therapist's waiting room. I wanted to show off how good I was. I wanted her to see that I was good at my job and that I was an important part of the company I worked for. Looking back, I'm not sure why I thought she would even care.

In the therapy sessions, things weren't any different. I wanted to be the best at being a client. I wanted my therapist to like me the best. Because of this, I never showed my true self, not that I could have if I wanted to, since I had no idea who my true self was. I said the things I thought I was supposed to say in therapy.

Years later, when I'd found myself a bit better and my true self was much sloppier than I would have ever liked to admit, I asked my therapist if she liked me better before, when I had looked more together. She told me no. She said that the show I would put on was a bit creepy and that she could see right through it.

After about six months of therapy, I broke down. I remember the entire situation very well. My doctor had just put me on Zoloft. I made sure she knew I wasn't depressed (depression was strictly forbidden in my "life rules"). She said sometimes antidepressants can help people with eating disorders, so I agreed to try them.

My dad was in town visiting from Boston where he and my mother had been living. Because my sister and I lived together in a small apartment in the Bay Area, he stayed at a hotel nearby. It was his birthday and we went to a San Francisco Giants baseball game to celebrate.

Throughout the entire game, I felt that something was deeply wrong, but I had no idea how to describe it. I made it through the game, telling people I wasn't feeling well when they asked. Somehow it worked out that my dad had his hotel room for an extra night longer than he needed, so I decided to stay in the room alone after he went home.

That night, for the first time in my life, I seriously considered suicide. I had a bottle full of Zoloft. I did not attempt suicide that night, but I did see a side of myself I'd never seen before. It was also the first time I ever self-harmed.

The next day, I went to an emergency appointment with my therapist that we'd set up the night before. At the end of the session she decided that I needed to be checked into a psychiatric hospital. Usually, this idea would have been so far beyond what was allowed in my rules that I would have faked happiness in order not to go. But I was past caring about anything. I was no longer making any decisions for myself. Something within me had taken the controls away from my brain and I had no choice but to follow along.

I spent my first day and night in the hospital heavily depressed. I had never been in a situation like this. I was scared, but for the most part, I didn't care. I wasn't there to make friends or learn about this new situation I'd been put in. I could barely focus on living.

I was put on a 72-hour hold (which is called a 5150 hold in California) and wasn't allowed to leave the hospital. We did art therapy and got to go outside every now and then.

Time went by slowly.

After the first day in the hospital, I started to feel better. I figured I had done the very worst thing possible: I had broken the image of myself that I felt the need to portray. Probably the only thing I could have done that was worse than going to a psychiatric hospital was getting arrested, but this felt equally as bad.

Once I realized that I'd done the worst thing, a feeling of lightness came over me. I felt like no matter what I did in life from that point on, I could always say: "well, at least I'm not in the psych hospital." It was a freedom that I couldn't explain. For the first time in my life I felt like I could do whatever I truly wanted. It was like I'd been freed from this jail I'd built for myself. I could work at a fast food restaurant, it would be better than being in the psych hospital. I could hitchhike around the world, again, better than being in the psych unit.

At the time, the doctors didn't believe that I felt better. But I didn't care what they thought. I loved the freedom I was feeling. The doctors all wanted me to stay in the hospital for longer than the 5150, but since I wasn't exhibiting signs of suicidal ideation anymore, they couldn't hold me against my will.

—

I left the hospital and quickly fell back into a deep depression. The high I had experienced turned itself around. Once the truth behind all the ridiculous rules had come to light, my house of cards fell and there was nothing left. I was a completely empty person.

As it turns out, my primary psychiatric problem was not my eating disorder. An eating disorder is often a symptom of a larger problem, not the problem itself. I had been using it as a crutch, as a way to deal with my larger issue. Once I broke down, the next symptom I started to experience was a deep depression. Again, this was not my main problem; it was another symptom. It wasn't until years later that I learned my true illness: borderline personality disorder (BPD).

There are many ways to describe BPD. Hollywood has portrayed people who suffer from BPD as psychotic. I have often felt a lot of shame in having this particular mental illness. It's not pretty. Its definition includes being manipulative and having extreme emotional mood swings. The way that I define it is a little different though.

The best way that I can explain BPD is the feeling of not

actually being a person. It had stripped away so much of myself that there was very little left of the real me.

Sure, I was still funny and smart, and most people would never know that there was anything wrong with me. But my intelligence and wit were calculated. Everything had a rule associated with it. Nothing about me was genuine. Everything I did had the end goal of getting people to like me. The irony was that people didn't like me all that much. I was forgettable.

I remember being baffled by how some people acted irrationally or were rude to others and still had friends. I now understand that we don't love each other because we are all perfect. Life is much more complicated than that.

—

While I couldn't understand what was happening to me, my therapist, on the other hand, knew exactly what she was doing, and she told me that my job was to just show up and try my best. I never once gave up on therapy. I often spent days and nights wanting to kill myself and yet I never missed a single session with my therapist.

I fell deeply depressed. Before my break down, I had been running marathons and was extremely productive. Afterwards, I had to take a three month leave of absence from my job. I never went back to that job. I tried a few times but I was much too ill.

I flew out to Boston to talk with my parents and tell them what was going on and ever since, they have done their best to support me. In fact, my dad met with my therapist and she recommended that I get a dog. I never would have thought of this because I could barely take care of myself.

But she knew that there were some tough times ahead in my life and that I needed a companion.

The next day, my dad took me to get a little Pekingese puppy he had found online. I instantly fell in love with my dog Luka. He's now 14 years old, sitting next to me as I write this book. He's one of the best things that's ever happened to me in my life.

Since I was on a leave of absence from work, I started going to a partial hospitalization program (PHP). I needed a reason to get out of bed in the morning so my therapist recommended I attend the daily sessions. I could barely keep myself together. I was extremely depressed and had almost completely given up on eating altogether. Eventually, my therapist recommended that I go to a residential treatment center.

I was sent to a treatment center in Arizona. I slept for the first three days I was there but eventually had to make an effort to participate in the program. I worked with the doctors to get my medication sorted out. I had been taken off the Zoloft immediately after my break down but had been struggling to find another medicine that could help alleviate my depression.

In the treatment center, I couldn't hide my eating disordered behaviors anymore. I couldn't skip meals, I couldn't make myself throw up, and I had to come face to face with the fact that I was severely ill. On top of this, my self-harming behaviors had increased, and I would often cut myself. I struggled along with the rest of my peers in the center but eventually, my depression lifted slightly, and my behaviors calmed down.

I learned a lot from my time in the treatment center. Most treatment centers host a family week, where members of each patient's family spend the week in therapy groups with the patient. Without fail, everyone I've ever met has described family week as extremely difficult. This was no exception for me. Having to confront my family and having them confront me about how each of our behaviors have been harmful to each other was hard.

However, our relationship has grown stronger because of that week. I was so touched that each of my family members took a break from their lives to be there for the entire week with me. I knew that not everyone was lucky enough to have people show up for them.

Time in the treatment center went by slowly. I struggled with depression and was often confrontational. I was angry and was not always able to accept help as it was offered. But I stumbled through and did the best I could. After three months, I was sent home in a better place emotionally. I was able to eat and didn't feel the need to purge after everything I ate.

—

Of course, this was not the end of my struggles. Far from it. Over the course of the next few years, I was sent back to the psychiatric hospital about a half a dozen times. I started to dissociate from myself which is a feeling I would describe as similar to getting high. This would happen to me without taking any drugs. I would lose myself. When this happened, I was unreachable to my therapist and she would often need to send me back to the psychiatric hospital. We had to work together to help me manage the dissociation.

I also still struggled with depression often and overdosed twice and had to be taken to the ER.

The first time I overdosed, I'd been very depressed for a while. My parents had moved from Boston to the San Francisco Bay Area and while I had an apartment of my own, I spent my days and nights at my parents' house. I slept on their couch all day long while my dad worked from home. One day, he had gone to a work meeting and I overdosed on pills. My therapist called me, I think to reschedule an appointment, and I told her what I'd done. She quickly called my father, and he returned home to take me to the ER.

The two of us spent the day in the ER while the staff watched over me. I had not taken a lethal amount of medicine and spent the day throwing up. In the evening, the ER staff sent me to a psych hospital. This was not new to me but since I didn't have insurance at the time, they struggled to find a hospital that would accept me. Finally, at around midnight, a couple of paramedics came to get me to take me to the John George hospital in Oakland, California.

John George is a psych hospital that accepts anyone, whether or not they have insurance. It is a dangerous facility that is overcrowded. The ambulance drivers and I waited for at least an hour in the parking lot, in line to get checked in. I was tired and just wanted to sleep. One of the paramedics looked at me and said: "don't be in a rush to get in there. And once you get in, stay out of dark corners and you should be fine." It was frightening.

Sure enough, the psych hospital was scary. After being checked in, I was sent to a large room where people were sleeping on mats on the ground. Someone told me to grab a mat and pick a spot. I knew I had no other choice but to comply, but it was horrifying.

Luckily, my dad and a doctor at John George spoke and

my dad agreed to take me home and watch me. Being released from a 5150 hold before the 72 hours are up is rare but in this situation, it was the best move for me.

My dad came to get me at 3 am and true to his word, he watched me over the next few days. He signed us both up for a gym membership at the local YMCA. Just getting to the gym was a win for me. I would rarely do much of a workout while I was there. I could do a few weight machines or swim a few laps. I wasn't getting in shape. I was struggling to leave the house. It was a massive difference from the college athlete/ marathoner I had once been.

—

The second time I overdosed on pills, I was completely out of my mind. I had been given a new prescription that I knew I wasn't reacting well to. I made an emergency appointment with my psychiatrist and he ignored my concerns. It was the day before he was going on vacation and he did not listen when I told him that I wasn't sleeping at all, I wasn't able to concentrate, and I was completely out of my mind. He was only focused on the fact that I was eating less. Since I'd been in recovery, I'd struggled to keep my weight down. I had quickly gained a lot of weight and this medicine was helping me manage my food intake.

I left the appointment feeling hopeless (and completely out of my mind). I went home and took a three-month supply of pills. When I realized what I'd done I asked my dad to take me to the hospital. Luckily for me, the hospital was only a couple of blocks away.

When I got to the ER and once I told the nurse how many pills I'd taken, she ran to get me help. Another nurse quickly came with activated charcoal for me to drink. Activated charcoal can counteract the effects of a drug overdose. I drank a little bit but wasn't keen on doing anything to help myself. I do not remember having a seizure, but I did.

I woke up a couple of days later in the intensive care unit (ICU) to the voices of my parents talking to a doctor. The doctor said: "she can hear you now, but she cannot move at all." He was right, I could hear them, but I was paralyzed. Then I heard my mom telling me how much she loved me. I willed myself to open my eyes or move my hand or something. I wanted to tell her that I'd heard her, that I was sorry, and that I loved her too. But I was completely paralyzed. The details of what happened to me in that ICU are still unclear to me. I don't know why I was paralyzed or what happened after I had a seizure. I do know that I was quite sick for the next few days.

Once I was physically better, around three days after my seizure, I was released from the ICU. Usually I would have had to go back to the psych hospital, but the doctors decided that this overdose occurred because I was not reacting well to a new medicine I had recently been put on, so I was allowed to go home.

—

Anytime I would be sent to the psych hospital, my life would be turned upside down in one way or another. It's hard to just not show up for work or school for a few days and not be able to explain what happened. I once was sent to the hospital after the second day of a new job. I couldn't explain to my boss where I was, so I had to quit the job. I would usually spend a lot of time being extremely depressed after going to the psych hospital. I would feel like a failure. I would want to give up.

I spent the next few years white-knuckling life, waiting for my next appointment with my therapist. We met Tuesdays and Thursdays, and my time in between was spent counting down the minutes until the next appointment.

While I was in therapy, I needed to work. On a whim, I applied to work as a preschool teacher and somehow I got the job. I was terrified. I've always loved kids but hadn't been around them in my late-teens, early twenties. I also worried that I might be doing a disservice to the kids I worked with since I felt like such a disaster.

My therapist had a 2 year old son and throughout the years often told me that she wished I could be her son's teacher or babysitter. She knew I would never put a child in danger and she always encourageed me to work with kids. I still worried but even as my sisters started to have kids, they always trusted me with their kids. Working with kids was such a joy and gift in my life.

—

For 12 years my therapist and I worked together and eventually life stopped being so hard for me. I still fell apart but those times were becoming fewer and farther between and my therapist and I worked together to help me manage myself when I did fall apart.

My therapist worked with me to save my life. Without her I would not be here today. I had no idea what I was even working on for most of the time we were working together. All I knew was that my job was to show up and trust her.

It was difficult work and oftentimes I felt like I would never feel better. In fact, I felt like that for years. I felt like I was in a dark tunnel and there was no light coming from anywhere. I couldn't see that there was an end to this undefinable hell I was going through.

The way my therapist and I talked about what I was going through was to imagine that I was Humpty Dumpty. I was just sitting up there on my wall hanging out. The next thing I knew, I would have a "great fall" and suddenly I would be lying on the ground in a million pieces. [For this analogy to work, ignore the part about the king's horses and men not being able to put Humpty together again.] The important part of the analogy is that there was often no reason for this fall off the wall. Out of nowhere, I would fall and then I would be in a million little pieces. My therapist and I would then have to work to put the pieces back together again.

It was really hard work. Initially, I couldn't even tell that I'd fallen apart. I didn't realize it. Falling apart would sometimes take the form of dissociation. Other times I would get really angry with my therapist. I would call her and yell or be unkind to her. For a long time, I wasn't present enough to be able to understand that I was even doing it. Eventually, I learned to recognize when it happened. Then, I needed to learn how to act when I did fall off the wall. Finally, I had to learn how not to fall off the wall at all.

All of this took years and was very painful work. In 2013, I was well enough to join a dialectical behavioral therapy (DBT) group. DBT focuses on the idea that two opposing things can be true at the same time and that the world will not fall apart because of it. In the group, I learned many techniques to help me stay on my wall.

—

Throughout my struggles, my parents and sisters helped

as much as they could. Mostly, all they could really do for me was just be there. And they were always there. My family has been there for me without fail whenever I've needed them. My parents have supported me and my sisters have both become my best friends. I have had support from some amazing friends over the years. Some people have been there for me throughout the years, while other friends are people that I may have lost touch with but that I know I could reach out to at any time. In the past few years, friendship has come to have a new meaning for me.

My recovery journey took 12 years. It's been 15 years since I first walked into my therapist's office, and honestly, I'm still learning. I've since moved to Denver and have started to work with a new therapist.

One day, in 2016, I realized that life wasn't as hard as it once had been for me. I didn't struggle every single day anymore. My therapist always told me that I wasn't crazy (even though I felt it) but that I was just tangled up inside. I still feel crazy sometimes, but I don't feel tangled very much anymore. Life makes sense and it's so much simpler than I ever made it out to be.

Even though I was doing better, I still had a lot of work to do. After so many years of ignoring what my true thoughts and beliefs were, I had no idea how I truly felt about anything. One afternoon, my new therapist was trying to make a point about something, and she needed an example from me. She said: "give me an example of a food you like." I'll never know the point of the exercise she was trying to take me through, because I got stuck on her question. At that moment in time, when I truly thought about it, I could not come up with a single food that I liked. My thoughts had been so hijacked by what I should or should not feel or think that the truth was lost to me.

I'm still learning what types of foods I like or what my favorite color is, but I'm getting there.

—

I've gone through many jobs, many nights in psychiatric hospitals, a foreclosure, a bankruptcy, loss of many friendships, and full years lost to mental illness. When I first started working with my therapist, she told me that what we were about to work through together was going to be the hardest thing I've ever done in my life. She was right.

Throughout the years, I often wished I hadn't opened this Pandora's box. I wished I would have stayed in my sad little world. It would have been easier by far.

Now, though, I get to enjoy life. I never thought I would get to do so. I have a job that is meaningful to me and that I love very much.

Sometimes I still struggle with feeling forgettable but I'm finding it harder and harder to believe that. I've noticed that as I've been putting myself out into the world, people have been responsive. I've taken risks in showing people that I care about them, and they've surprised me by caring about me right back. For example, I used to work out of a co-working space called Progress Coworking but had to stop going for financial reasons. After a few months away, the owners reached out and personally invited me to come back at no cost. I was shocked.

I still have down days, but I've developed a lot of coping skills and I've gotten better at using them when needed. My most helpful coping skills involve reaching out to others. Sometimes this means texting a friend I haven't heard from for a long while just to check in. Other times,

I'll reach out to my best friends for a more in-depth conversation. I also spend time with my family; my niece and nephews offer a great distraction and I love them more than anything.

I have found that imagining my emotions as waves has been extremely helpful for me. Sadness will always come into my life at some point. I'm okay with that. I actually welcome it, as I know it means that I'm able to feel emotions and I know that sadness is a part of life. What helps me is to view my sadness as a wave coming in and going out. In fact, all my emotions are like that. If I'm happy, I know that I can enjoy my happiness while it's here and that it will leave at some point. The comforting thing is that I know the happiness will come back.

Familiarity and routine are also very helpful for me. I can get thrown off very easily by any type of change. In order to counter this, I have a long list of familiar things that help keep me steady. The best example is a morning radio show that I listen to every day. The year I moved to California in the mid-90s, San Francisco got a new radio station, which also marked the start of the Sarah and Vinnie morning show. The radio show has been on air ever since. Even though I've since left California, I can now listen to their show on a podcast. Their dependability has offered me much comfort for more than 20 years.

I've also set up routines that I try to stick to, sometimes with more success than others. I try to wake up at the same time every day, and I try to make sure my days are structured similarly every day. My dad and I even have lunch together every Friday.

I find comfort in familiar clothing, books, and even a morning cup of coffee. Sometimes I even carry around a small object, so I have something tangible to stabilize myself. In fact, in my wallet, I carry around a piece of paper from my old therapist. If anyone ever found it, it would look like garbage, but I know its meaning.

I now have some amazing friends. My circle of friends is slightly unusual because they live all around the world but there are a few awesome people that I know I could call anytime. They also know that they could call me anytime.

In a recent conversation with a friend, I realized that I've taken up a lot of creative hobbies in the past few years. Two years ago, I decided I wanted to build a teardrop trailer. The last thing I'd built was a birdhouse in woodshop in the seventh grade, but I was all in. I loved building that trailer. It was difficult and I made a lot of mistakes, but it gave me such a feeling of accomplishment that it was worth every splinter. I've also discovered my creative side in other ways. For example, for the last nine years, I've been organizing an annual family run, for which I design custom patches. I've learned that I am competent and that there is nothing wrong with the person I am.

I've also started to workout again. I am cautious to work-out only for fun, as I know I can easily get carried away. I've found a new pool that I love. Recently, I was swimming laps and someone stopped me and asked me why I'd pushed off the wall and dove straight to the bottom of the pool. He thought it was some workout strategy. I told him that I was just having fun. I sometimes swim like I did when I was 7 years old. I was reminded of the days I would barely have the energy to swim a couple of laps at the YMCA years ago. I'm proud of how far I've come.

—

I missed out on a lot throughout my twenties. Because of my illness, I'm not married and don't have children (both of which I would love). I don't own a house, have a high-paying job, or even much of a savings account. But I do have my life back. I have a personality. I have opinions that sometimes clash with others. There are people I choose to be friends with and there are people that I choose not to be friends with.

I'm not sure that I'll ever say I'm recovered from my struggle with mental illness. And I don't want to say that. If I say I've recovered, I think I will be less likely to recognize a slip-up or a step backwards. I also recognize that there will be times where things are harder. Mental illness will be part of my life forever. It's not a path I asked for and it's not one I wish on anyone else, but I have accepted it as part of who I am, and I am proudly in recovery!

Tips from participants

In writing this book, I asked each of the participants which coping skills have worked for them. I've compiled their tips here:

Connections

When I asked this book's participants what has helped them the most in their recovery, by far the most common answer was staying connected with others. This looks different for everyone. For example, participants said they connected with:
- a community within a sports team.
- people who have experienced the same thing(s) they have.
- a spouse or significant other.
- friends and family.
- a pet.

In addition to having connections, being able to be vulnerable and share with those connections is invaluable. Participants mentioned the importance of:
- communicating their needs.
- reaching out when in need.
- showing weakness.

Structure

Creating a structure or routine was another highly recommended tip from participants. Some people found that having a pet helped them set up a routine, as pets need to be taken care of. Joining a club, sport, or community can help, too.

Health

Many participants said that focusing on their health in specific ways has been helpful.[14] They suggested:
- getting plenty of sleep.
- practicing yoga.
- practicing self-care.
- reducing caffeine consumption.
- getting away from using food as a weapon and instead using it to help oneself function at maximum capacity.
- following body-positive models on social media.
- take a break from social media when needed.

Distraction

Sometimes distraction offers a way to get out of your current state of mind. Distraction is a short-term solution, but can be very helpful nonetheless. Some distraction methods participants suggested are:
- drawing or coloring.
- taking a walk or shower.
- going out with people.
- going to places you've never been.
- spending time outdoors.
- laying down under a favorite comforter.
- making tea.

Whatever it is, find a distraction that isn't destructive and that works for you.

---

14   Note: Many participants in this book have suffered from eating disorders. These tips are only suggestions. If you are suffering from an eating disorder, please speak with a therapist and/or dietician.

Therapy/Groups

While not all participants were seeing a therapist when I spoke with them, all had done so at one point in time. Other than traditional therapy, participants recommended Alcoholics Anonymous or other 12-step programs like Eating Disorders Anonymous. Some participants also saw dieticians.

Participants found that applying the tools they learned in therapy has been helpful. Examples they provided were:
- exposure therapy.
- using the "catch it, challenge it, change it" approach.
- "playing the tape forward": before taking an action, think about why you are going to do it and ask yourself if it will help you get closer to your goal.
- imagining your emotions as waves: all waves come and go, so no matter what emotion you are feeling, it will not last forever.
- accepting that it is impossible to please everyone.
- accepting that it is okay to be sad, upset, or angry.
- allowing yourself to feel and experience all your emotions.
- catching yourself and recognizing when you're catastrophizing or doing "all or nothing" thinking.
- reminding yourself of what's important to you in life.
- recognizing that you have to want to get better.
- focusing on what you want to do and what it will take for you to get there.

- keeping grounded by slowing down and not looking too far into the future.
- talking about your struggles, whether to friends or in front of an audience (e.g. at a local school).

None of these suggestions are meant to be a substitute for getting professional help, nor are they intended to be prescriptive.

Book recommendations

During the interviews, almost every participant recommended a book or two. I decided to add these recommendations at the end of this book. Here are the books participants found helpful for their recovery:

General Psychology

1. "Radical Acceptance: Embracing Your Life with the Heart of a Buddha" by Tara Brach
2. "Rising Strong: How the Ability to Reset Transforms the Way We Live, Love, Parent, and Lead" by Brené Brown
3. "Braving the Wilderness: The Quest for True Belonging and the Courage to Stand Alone" by Brené Brown
4. "Wishful Drinking" by Carrie Fisher

Eating Disorders

1. "Life Without Ed: How One Woman Declared Independence from Her Eating Disorder and How You Can Too" by Jenni Schaefer

Borderline Personality Disorder

1. "Get Me Out of Here: My Recovery from Borderline Personality Disorder" by Rachel Reiland

Cognitive Behavioral Therapy

1. "Feeling Good: The New Mood Therapy" by
    David D. Burns
2. "Overcoming Unwanted Intrusive Thoughts:
    A CBT-Based Guide to Getting Over
    Frightening, Obsessive, or Disturbing
    Thoughts" by Sally M. Winston and Martin
    N. Seif

Poetry

1. "When the Fat Girl Gets Skinny" (YouTube
    video) by Blythe Baird
2. "Breath of Water: A Collection of Poems,
    Thoughts, and Irrational Feelings" by
    Caitlin Leigh
3. "Hollow Bone" by Caitlin Leigh
4. "Just Passing Through: From a Suicidal Mind
    to a Heart of Truth" by Caitlin Leigh

Image credits

All images have been reprinted with the permission of each participant with the following exceptions which are all licensed under creative commons:

- Cover image: Steiner Engeland via Unsplash https://unsplash.com/photos/UtEUUNHvMLs
- p. 71: Caleb Jones via Unsplash https://unsplash.com/photos/J3JMyXWQHXU
- p. 107: Peter Bucks via Unsplash https://unsplash.com/photos/oqon-nqUJ9Q
- p. 129: Farsai Chaikulngamdee via Unsplash https://unsplash.com/photos/L2wq7Y3h7ag

Acknowledgements

I've been working on this book for over two years and am so thankful to so many people who helped make this project a reality. First, thank you to each participant in this project for taking the time and for opening themselves up by retelling difficult stories. Thank you to my family for their unwavering support, for helping with editing, and offering their opinions whenever I asked. Thank you to my amazing friends, my therapists (past and present), and the myriad of amazing people that helped me throughout my recovery: From nutritionists, therapists in treatment centers, nurses, nurse-techs, doctors, admin staff. Your hard work has not gone unnoticed. I am here today because of you. Thank you!

Thanks to Diane Szulecki for editing the book. And thank you to all the people who donated to the Kickstarter for this book specifically Ric and Deb Pankrat, Lyndsay Koch, Beverly Lamberson, and Wayne Critchley. With the over 30 donations I received, I was able to travel around North America to meet with each participant. Thank you!

About the author

Courtney Pankrat holds a master's degree in psychology from John F. Kennedy University and a master's degree in sport management from the University of San Francisco. She works as the editor and communications manager for Shareable.net. She has been writing since 2011. This is her first book.

She currently lives in Denver, Colorado with her dog Luka.